I0024535

Albert Orville Wright

An Analysis and Exposition

of the Constitution of the State of Wisconsin

Albert Orville Wright

An Analysis and Exposition
of the Constitution of the State of Wisconsin

ISBN/EAN: 9783337119652

Printed in Europe, USA, Canada, Australia, Japan

Cover: Foto ©Suzi / pixelio.de

More available books at **www.hansebooks.com**

AN

ANALYSIS AND EXPOSITION

OF THE

CONSTITUTION OF THE STATE OF WISCONSIN,

DESIGNED

FOR THE USE OF TEACHERS, ADVANCED CLASSES IN SCHOOLS
AND CITIZENS GENERALLY.

BY A. O. WRIGHT.

" That which contributes most to preserve the State is to educate children with reference to the
State ; for the most useful laws, and most approved by every statesman, will be of no service, if
the citizens are not accustomed to and brought up in the principles of the Constitution "—ARISTO-
TLE, Politics, Book V, ch. 9.

MADISON, WIS.:
ATWOOD & CULVER, PUBLISHERS.
1873.

PREFACE.

THE reason for the existence of this little book is to be found in the amendment to our school law, enacted by the legislature of 1871, which requires the constitution of the United States and of the state of Wisconsin to be taught in our common schools, and studied by our teachers in order to receive certificates.

The object of this law is to acquaint our citizens with the principles of our government and the machinery used in carrying it on. The only way in which this knowledge of our civil government can be enforced, by law, is through our common schools and their teachers. Directly, this law affects only the teachers and pupils in our public schools; but, indirectly, it reaches a great number of parents and friends whose attention is called to the subject through them.

The author hopes that this little work will supply the demand thus created for a short and simple exposition of the constitution of this state, which shall unfold the principles and philosophy of our government, as well as explain the legal phraseology of the constitution, and which shall be adapted for school use, while at the same time it may be a convenient hand book of study and reference for those citizens who care to study the theory of their government.

For the benefit of students an analysis of the whole constitution, and of each article is given. For the benefit of teachers some suggestions upon the methods of teaching the constitution are given in an appendix. For the benefit of citizens, abstracts of those decisions of the supreme court which interpret the constitution, are given in foot notes. These abstracts are usually quoted from Simmons' Digest, but every reference has been carried back to the original reports of the supreme court, and wherever Simmons' abstract did not answer the purpose of this work a new one has been made. Every effort has been made to secure absolute accuracy in the references to these decisions. In order to give the text of the constitution as it now is, the amendments are inserted in their proper places, while the sections amended are given in the original form in the foot notes; and those parts of the constitution which have expired by their own limitation or which are indirectly abolished by amendments are enclosed in brackets, except in the case of the first legislative apportionment, given in article XIV, section 12, which, because of its length, is omitted.

In the preparation of this work a prime object has been to make it concise and, therefore, cheap in price, so as to bring it within the means of every voter and of every teacher and advanced pupil in our schools. It has not been possible within these limits, therefore, to answer every collateral question that could be asked about matters referred to in this constitution. Readers of this work are referred to the Legislative Manual, to the statutes of the state or to any good lawyer for answers to such questions.

The thanks of the author are due to Gen. SAMUEL FALLOWS, state superintendent of public instruction, for the first suggestion of the plan of this work, and for much valuable assistance and counsel since. His thanks are also due to H. H. HATCH, Esq., of New Lisbon, one of the soundest lawyers in this state, for much valuable help, especially upon articles I and VII, where a clear knowledge of legal terms and methods is most needed.

TABLE OF CONTENTS.

———

GENERAL ANALYSIS

OF THE

CONSTITUTION OF WISCONSIN.

THE GOVERNMENT OF WISCONSIN.

CONSTITUTION OF WISCONSIN.

We, [1]the people of Wisconsin, [2]grateful to Almighty God for our freedom, [3]in order to secure its blessings, [4]form a more perfect government, [5]insure domestic tranquillity and [6]promote the general welfare, do establish this constitution.

This preamble is plainly taken from the preamble to the United States constitution, with some changes. Notice the order in which the objects of the constitution are given: First *freedom*, then *government*, and then the two great ends of government, *domestic* tranquillity and the *general welfare*.

[1]The people are the source of all political power in Wisconsin, and "the people of Wisconsin" establish this constitution. Thus the very first words of the constitution show the republican form of government in this state, which is guaranteed to all the states by the United States constitution. This constitution is not granted by a monarch who can take it away again when he pleases; nor is it established by a few nobles for their own benefit. Here, in America, we are all sovereigns, and make laws and constitutions to suit ourselves. And, therefore, the preamble states that it is *the people* of Wisconsin who make this constitution.

[2]It is very proper for the people of the state in framing the constitution to express their thanks to God. This does not establish any religion, for this constitu-

tion (Art. I, sects. 18 and 19) guarantees complete freedom of religion. But it does mean this: That the people of Wisconsin believe in God and worship Him; and believe, moreover, that they owe their freedom to Him.

³The first and greatest object of Americans always is "to secure the blessings of freedom." And in accordance with this, the first article of our state constitution is a declaration of rights, intended to secure the blessings of freedom to every person in Wisconsin, citizen or foreigner, of whatever color, race, age or sex. And then the constitution goes on to arrange the machinery of government, so as to "insure domestic tranquillity and promote the general welfare."

'To secure the blessings of freedom, we need a settled government with good laws, justly carried out. It is not enough to be free ; we must be protected in our freedom from being oppressed by any one else ; and this can only be done by a regular and a just government.

Before this constitution was adopted and the state admitted to the union, the government of Wisconsin was territorial. It was a territory of the United States, and it was governed by the United States. The governor and judges of the territory were appointed by the President, and the laws passed by the territorial legislature could be overruled at any time by Congress, and, indeed, Congress could, if it pleased, have abolished the legislature altogether, and itself made laws for the territory. But when this constitution was adopted and Congress had made the territory of Wisconsin a state, with this constitution as its fundamental law, "a more perfect government " was formed. Within the limits fixed by the United States constitution, the people of the state can now manage their government to suit themselves. The state government is "a more perfect government" than the territorial government was.

'A good government will "insure the domestic tranquility" by preventing riots and insurrection, by restraining crimes of every kind, and by defending the state against war or invasion. And these things the constitution provides for.

'Besides these, a good government will "promote the general welfare" by promoting education, by fostering agriculture, manufactures and commerce, and by securing to every man, woman and child in the state, a fair chance in life. These things the constitution provides for either directly or indirectly. And thus the constitution fulfills the objects set forth in this preamble, as we shall see by the farther study of it.

ARTICLE I.

DECLARATION OF RIGHTS.

SECTION I.

[1]All men are born equally free and independent, and [2]have certain inherent rights; among these are life, liberty, and the pursuit of happiness. [3]To secure these rights, governments are instituted among men, deriving their just powers from the consent of the governed.*

[1] All men are born equally free and independent; but freedom and independence do not consist in having a

---

* This section is taken with very slight change, from the Declaration of Independence. Compare the following extract from that document with the section of the constitution of Wisconsin, given above:
"We hold these truths to be self-evident, that all men are created equal, that they are endowed by their Creator with certain inalienable rights, that among these are life, liberty and the pursuit of happiness, that to secure these rights, governments are instituted among men, deriving their just powers from the consent of the governed."

voice in the government, but only in being justly ruled and protected by a government of our own choice.

² There are two kinds of rights, *inherent rights* and *conventional rights.* Inherent rights are those rights that belong to everybody everywhere, and which it is the business of the law always to secure. Conventional rights are those that are given by law or by custom that has the force of law; and since they are given by law, they can be repealed by law. Inherent rights can be taken away by law, unjustly; for laws are not always just. Conventional rights may justly be taken away by law; for what the law has given, the law can take away.

For instance, the right to vote is a conventional right. The constitution, for various reasons, forbids certain persons to vote — women, children, persons who have come into the state within a year, wild Indians, convicts, United States soldiers and sailors. These persons cannot complain that the principle stated in this section has been violated; for the right to vote is not an inherent, but a conventional right. The people of the state, should they see fit, can extend the right to vote to any or all of these classes; or, if they see fit, can still further restrict the right to vote by shutting out other classes, and no one can reasonably complain. But if, because of the restriction or the extension of the suffrage, the inherent rights of any class are put in danger, they can rightfully complain; not because of that restriction or extension of the suffrage, but because of the consequences that flow from it in violation of their inherent rights.

Again, the right to hold property, subject to a reasonable taxation from the state, is an inherent right.

The government has no right to take any one's property from him without paying him for it, or to let any one else take it from him at all without his consent. A man has always the right to his earnings ; for it is with them that he buys the means of life and happiness, and it is the business of government to protect him in that right. But nobody has an *inherent right* to some particular kind of property ; like land, for instance. The owner-ship of land is only a conventional right, and, therefore, the state reserves to itself, in Article IX, the right of " em-inent domain," and will take a man's land whenever it is needed for a street or any other public purpose, whether he is willing to let it go or not. But, though the state can thus justly break through his conventional right to hold land, it cannot justly take away his inherent right to his property, and, therefore, the Constitution pro-vides (I, 13) that whenever the state takes away any-one's land, it must pay him a fair price for it.

These examples will show the distinction between in-herent and conventional rights, which must be kept carefully in mind all through this article. The object of this Declaration of Rights, with which our State Constitution so nobly begins, is to secure the *inherent* rights of every person who comes within the jurisdic-tion of the State. The line between inherent and con-ventional rights is very carefully and ably drawn. And it is to secure these rights by some power stronger than a bit of printed paper that the machinery of the state government was established in the rest of the consti-tution.

'The end of all government is to secure us in our indi-vidual freedom. A government that does not do this, is not worth having. The first duty of every government, whether it is that of a king, of a few nobles, or of the people, is to secure the subjects or citizens of that government in those inherent rights, without which they cannot be truly free. The right to life, to personal liberty, to have a fair chance in life, and to seek our happiness as we please, so long as we do not infringe on the rights of any one else, are inherent rights. To secure them is the object of all government. There is no peculiar sacredness in any institutions of government. They are but the means by which the end of good government is attained. Any form of government needs the consent of those who are governed, and, if it becomes oppressive, they have a right to change it. Acting on this principle, expressed in the Declaration of Independence,* the founders of American liberty revolted from the English government and established one of their own. And should the government of this State ever become oppressive and unjust, the people of the State will, doubtless, change it — peaceably if they can, forcibly if they must.

SECTION II.

¹There shall be neither slavery nor involuntary servitude in this state, ²other than for the punishment for crime, whereof the party shall have been duly convicted.

¹When the state constitution was adopted, African slavery was allowed in many states of our union, and it was, therefore, necessary for the state of Wisconsin to

---

*"That to secure these rights governments are instituted among men, deriving their just powers from the consent of the governed; and that whenever any form of government becomes destructive of these ends, it is the right of the people to alter or abolish it, and to institute a new government, laying its foundation on such principles, and organizing its powers in such form as to them shall seem most likely to effect their safety and happiness."

put itself on one side or the other of this question. This state prohibited slavery by this section. This provision in our state constitution is now made needless by the thirteenth amendment to the United States constitution, which prohibits slavery everywhere in the United States, and, of course, in Wisconsin as well as elsewhere ; so that now, even if the people of Wisconsin should repeal this section, that would not bring slavery here*.

Slavery violates the inherent right to liberty and the pursuit of happiness, and is, therefore, prohibited justly and consistently with section I. of this article.

²A person may be shut up in the state's prison, and thus have his liberty taken away, whenever he shows that he is a dangerous character by doing some crime. *His* right to liberty and the pursuit of happiness is taken away from him for these reasons : to stop him for a time from infringing on other people's rights, to reform him, if possible, and to prevent others from committing like crimes, by fear of a like penalty.

SECTION III.

Every person may ¹freely speak, write and publish his sentiments on all subjects, ²being responsible for the abuse of that right, and no laws shall be passed to restrain or abridge the liberty of speech or of the press. ³In all criminal prosecutions or indictments for libel, the truth may be given in evidence; and if it shall appear to the jury that the matter charged as libelous be true, and was published with good motives and for justifiable ends, the party shall be acquitted, ⁴and the jury shall have the right to determine the law and the fact.

¹Next to the right to life and to liberty of body, is the liberty of speech. In most countries it has been thought that it is not safe to let people speak or write what they

*The wording of the thirteenth amendment to the U. S. constitution is plainly taken from this section and other similar sections in the constitutions of other states, and from the Ordinance of 1787.

please. But in the United States the people govern, and, therefore, we are not afraid to allow free speech. In Wisconsin, as in the rest of our country, everybody can speak or write or print whatever he pleases, with one exception, named in this section.

²We have found out in America that the truth will take care of itself, if we only let it alone and give it a fair chance; and that the more we try to help the truth by law, the more we really hurt it. Freedom is the best atmosphere for truth to live in. Tennyson's words in praise of England are just as true of America:

> "It is the land that freemen till,
>   That sober-suited Freedom chose;
>   The land where, girt with friends or foes,
>   A man may speak the thing he will;

> "Where faction seldom gathers head;
>   But by degrees to fullness wrought,
>   The strength of some diffusive thought
> Hath time and space to work and spread."

The liberty of speech is limited by the rights of other people. If we were free to say anything we chose, we might harm other people very greatly. Therefore, although we may speak our minds, we must not do it so as to injure any one's reputation.* This is the rule of the English common law, which would be our own law on the subject, were it not for the rest of this section, as the common law is adopted by this constitution (XIV, 13).

²Under the common law, the rule was "the greater the truth, the greater the libel."

*"A libel is a malicious publication, either by printing or writing, or by signs or pictures, which accuses a person of a crime, or blackens his character, or tends to expose him to public ridicule, contempt or hatred." (Simmons' Digest, p. 481. Wis. Reports, vol. iv., p. 231.)

"An action for libel may be sustained for words *published*, which tend to bring the plaintiff into public hatred, contempt or ridicule, even though the same words *spoken* would not have been actionable." (Simmons' Digest, p. 431. Wis. Reports, vol. ix, p. 540.)

B

But under this section of our constitution, any one may tell that which will injure the reputation of another, on certain conditions: First, it must be true.* Second, the one who tells it must tell it with good motives — that is, not maliciously or spitefully. Third, he must tell it for justifiable ends, that is, not for the sake of hurting some one's reputation, but to do some good.

Under this provision of our constitution, an editor may warn his readers against swindlers by name, or publish the names and actions of any wrongdoers; any one may tell a District Board that a certain teacher is unfit to teach, or tell a merchant that his clerk is stealing from the money-drawer, or publish charges against public officers, and so on through an endless variety of cases.

'Usually, the judge determines the law, and the jury the facts in the case; but in libel suits, under this section, the jury decide everything — the fact whether the thing charged was actually said, or written, or printed, and the law whether the thing charged is a libel within the meaning of the law. By this it is not meant that the judge has nothing to say about the law; he instructs the jury as to what the law is, and then the jury decide for themselves.

SECTION IV.

The right of the people [1]peaceably to assemble to consult for the common good, and [2]to petition the government or any department thereof, shall never be abridged.

---

* "In order to justify in such a case, it is not sufficient to show that the libelous matter was previously published by a third person, and that the defendant, at the time he published it, disclosed the name of such person, and believed all its statements to be true; but he must aver and prove that the plaintiff was actually guilty of the matters reported to have been charged against him, just as he would be required to do if he had charged such plaintiff directly with actual guilt." [Simmons' Digest, p. 481, Wis. Reports, vol. xiv, p. 663.]

[1]In many countries, the government is afraid to let the people have political meetings or get up petitions for the redress of grievances. Here, any number of people may come together in any sort of societies, religious, social or political, or even in treasonable conspiracies, and, so long as as they behave themselves and do not hurt any body or make any great disturbance, they may express themselves in public meetings by speeches and resolutions as they choose.

[2]There are very few countries in which the government is so despotic that it refuses to receive petitions and to hear the complaints of its subjects or citizens. And ours being a free government, of course gives this right to its citizens. If any person or persons wish to have the laws changed in any way, they have a right to petition the legislature for that change. The legislature must receive and listen to the petition, and then it may make the change in the laws, or not, as the members may see fit. So also with city councils and county, village, town and district boards. On all things that are under their care, they *must* receive and listen to all petitions that anybody chooses to send them; and then they may do as they please about acting on them. So, also, for anything that is in charge of any executive or judicial officer. The Governor *must* receive all petitions for pardon, but he can do as he chooses about granting the pardon.

SECTION V

[1]The right of trial by jury shall remain inviolate; [2]and shall extend to all cases at law, without regard to the amount in controversy; [3]but a jury trial may be waived by the parties in all cases, in the manner prescribed by law.

'Trial by jury is an ancient English custom that was meant to secure fair trials, so that the decision should not depend upon the judge alone, but also upon a number of unprejudiced citizens. With the rest of the English common law, trial by jury was brought over to this country by the English colonists, and has been adopted in every state in our Union. The constitution therefore says that the right of trial by jury shall remain inviolate.*

A jury generally consists of twelve persons chosen in such a way that they shall be impartial.† In suits before a justice of the peace, the number is usually six. In any verdict of a jury, all must agree.

²Under the United States constitution, trial by jury is guaranteed in all criminal cases (III, 2) and in all civil suits where the value in controversy shall exceed twenty dollars (Amendment VII.). Under this section the right of trial by jury is extended to all cases at law. Equity cases are decided by the judge alone.‡

---

*"The provision in our state constitution (I. 5), that 'the right of trial by jury' shall remain inviolate,' refers to that right as it then existed, and means that it shall remain as full and perfect after the adoption of the constitution as it was at the time of its adoption." (Simmons' Digest, p. 446; Wis. Reports, Vol. i., p. 401; Vol. ii., p. 22; Vol. vi., p. 503; Vol. xvi., p. 461)

†"The common-law writers applied the term 'trial by jury' only to a trial by a jury of twelve men, and that was the legal number of jurors for the trial of all issues of fact in all courts of record in Wisconsin, at the time of the adoption of the constitution, except in cases where the parties consented to a different number; and the right to a trial by a jury of twelve is the right preserved and secured by the constitution." (Simmons' Digest, p. 447; Wis. Reports, Vol. ii., p. 22; Vol. iii., p. 219.

The "courts of record" now in existence in this state are the supreme and circuit courts and the county courts, so far as they have jurisdiction of "cases at law." The courts of justices of the peace are not courts of record.

"An alien who has declared his intention to become a citizen, but has never been fully naturalized so as to be a citizen of the United States, is not a competent juror." (Simmons' Digest, p. 446: Wis. Reports, Vol. v., p. 324; Vol. xvii., p. 674.)

‡"The right of trial by jury does not extend to equity cases, in which by the law and practice existing at the time the constitution was adopted, the parties were not as a matter of right entitled to a jury trial." (Simmons' Digest, p. 447; Wis. Reports, Vol. xiv., p. 461.)

[1]A jury trial may be waived by a criminal when he pleads "guilty" in open court. There is no need of a jury to establish his guilt, since he has himself confessed it in a regular and lawful way. In criminal cases, the jury can determine only the fact, and that *is* determined when the plea of "guilty" is put in, and therefore no jury is needed to determine it.

In civil suits, a jury trial may be waived where both parties agree to it. In cases brought before a justice of the peace, the presumption is that a jury will not be wished, and the case will be tried without one unless either party call for a jury. In that case, the call cannot be denied, under this section of the constitution. In civil suits before a judge, the presumption is that a jury is wished, and the case will be tried before a jury unless both parties agree to waive it.

SECTION VI.

[1]Excessive bail shall not be required, nor [2]shall excessive fines be imposed, nor [3]cruel and unusual punishment inflicted.

[1]Bail is the security given that a person arrested for any offense will appear in court and stand his trial when the time comes. When no bail is given, the person charged with the offense will be kept in jail till his trial comes off; not to punish him, for that is unlawful, under section 2; for he has not yet been "duly convicted" of any crime, but to make sure that he will be on hand to be tried. Should a justice of the peace ask too great bail, the case can be carried before a circuit or county judge or a court commissioner, (VII, 23,) on a writ of

* This is copied, word for word, from the United States Constitution, (Amendment VIII) with two trifling exceptions that do not change the sense.

habeas corpus, and the bail be reduced by him, should he think it is excessive. If a circuit judge asks too great bail, the case would be carried in the same way before the supreme court.

[2] Fines and punishments are prescribed by law for each offense. The law prescribes the greatest and the least fine or other punishment, and the court must not impose a greater punishment than the greatest, or a less one than the least prescribed by law. If the law, itself, should fix too severe a penalty, the judge could decide that the law is unconstitutional, and refuse to punish the offender so heavily. No such case, however, has yet arisen in this state.

[3] Cruel and unusual punishments are understood to mean such punishments as whipping, branding with a hot iron, maiming, torturing, burning at the stake, breaking on the wheel, drawing and quartering, and the like. These were, until a century or two ago, inflicted everywhere; but have now been abolished in all civilized countries.

SECTION VII.

In all criminal prosecutions, the accused shall enjoy the right [1]to be heard by himself and counsel, to demand the nature and cause of the accusation against him, [3]to meet the witnessess face to face; [4]to have compulsory process to compel the attendance of witnesses in his behalf; and in prosecutions by indictment or information, to a [5]speedy [6]public trial [7]by an impartial jury of the county or district wherein the offense shall have been committed; which county or district shall have been previously ascertained by law.

This section is like Amendment VI to the United States Constitution. The object is the same in both — to secure a fair trial to accused persons; but the particular means of doing that, though the same in both, are arranged in a different order. The following is an analysis of either:

ACCUSED PERSONS SHALL HAVE A FAIR TRIAL.	1. By knowing of what they are accused.	
	2. By having a trial,	1. Speedy,
		2. Public,
		3. By an impartial jury,
		4. In the district where the offense was committed.
	3. By having fair testimony,	1. By cross-examining the opposing witnesses,
		2. By subpœnaing their own witnesses.
	4. By having heard in person or by counsel.	

¹Every person has a right to be his own lawyer if he chooses. But most persons will always prefer to have a lawyer to carry on the case for them, who is skilled in the technicalities of law, who knows how things are done in a court-room, and who can talk. As the law used to be in England, an accused person was not allowed a lawyer, while the state had the best lawyers to plead the case against him.

This section of the constitution prevents any such injustice. Every accused person can have a lawyer if he chooses. If he is too poor to furnish one himself, the judge appoints one for him, who is paid by the county or state. And every accused person has also the right to speak for himself, if he chooses, after the lawyers are through.

²An accused person always has a right to see the indictment against him, and to know for what offense he is to be tried, so that he may be prepared to defend himself as well he can ; and, if he is innocent, so that he can prove his innocence.

³He has the right to meet the witnesses face to face, so that he or his lawyer may cross-examine them to see whether they tell the truth or not.

⁴ He may *subpœna* witnesses for himself, as the state can against him, so that if any one knows anything about a crime, he may be compelled to come into court and testify, so that the truth may be got at as near as may be.

⁵ The trial for petty offenses, before a justice of the peace, comes as soon as possible. For graver crimes, the trial comes off at the next term of the circuit court, in the county, unless there is some good reason for putting it off.

⁶ Trials are always public, and any one can be present who pleases. It is more likely that justice will be done in this way than if the trials were held privately.

⁷ An impartial jury is secured by the names of jurors being drawn by lot from lists prepared some time beforehand. Then, each party to a suit or trial has the right to challenge a certain number of jurors peremptorily, and any number for cause. That is, either party may have so many persons stricken off the jury without giving any reason for it; and either party may have as many more persons stricken off the jury as are disqualified to act as jurors under the laws. When a person is tried for an offense punishable by imprisonment for life, he is entitled to twenty-four peremptory challenges, and the prosecuting attorney to six. In other criminal cases, the accused is entitled to four peremptory challenges, and the prosecuting attorney to the same number. In civil cases, each party is entitled to three peremptory challenges. Challenges for cause may be for a variety of reasons; but the main cause is that the juror is prejudiced or has formed an opinion upon the case.

SECTION VIII.

[1]*No person shall be held to answer for criminal offense without due process of law,* [2]and no person, for the same offense, shall be put twice in jeopardy of punishment, [3]nor shall be compelled in any criminal case to be a witness against himself. [4]All persons shall before conviction be bailable by sufficient sureties, except for capital offenses when the proof is evident or the presumption great; [5]and the privilege of the writ of *habeas corpus* shall not be suspended unless when in cases of rebellion or invasion the public safety may require it.*

[1]" Due process of law " now means, either a preliminary examination before a justice of the peace, or information laid before the district attorney. The object of this, as of the old way of indictment by a grand jury, is to prevent evil-disposed persons annoying innocent people with frivolous or groundless accusations. No person can be held to answer for a criminal charge, unless it can be shown that there is probable reason to suppose that he is guilty. If it were not so, an enemy might trump up charges against any one of us, without any proof, and hurt our reputation, and put us to a great deal of expense and trouble, all for nothing.

In time of war, martial law takes the place of civil law for all soldiers and sailors, and all the people who live where the war is going on. When nations are fighting, they cannot stop for the slow justice of peace. In time

*This section was amended at the general election, Nov. 18, 1870, so as to abolish the grand jury system. Before it was amended it read as follows, putting the words in italics below, in the place of those in italics above:

" *No person shall be held to answer for a criminal offense, unless on the presentment or indictment of a grand jury, except in cases of impeachment, or in cases cognizable by justices of the peace, or arising in the army or navy, or in the militia when in actual service in time of war or public danger;* and no person for the same offense shall be put twice in jeopardy of punishment nor shall be compelled in any criminal case to be a witness against himself. All persons shall before conviction be bailable by sufficient sureties, except for capital offenses when the proof is evident or the presumption great; and the privileges of the writ of *habeas corpus* shall not be suspended unless when, in cases of rebellion or invasion, the public safety may require."

As this section originally read, it was taken, with some slight changes, from the U. S. Constitution. [Amendment V, and Art. I, Sec. 9, Clause 2.]

of peace, soldiers and sailors can be punished by the courts for all offenses against the laws; and also by their officers or by court martial, for all offenses against the army regulations. In such cases, martial or military law is considered " due process of law."

² No person can be tried twice for the same offense; but, if the jury disagree, he can be tried before a new jury. That is not another trial, but the same one continued. Or, the case may be carried to a higher court on an appeal, or a writ of *certiorari* or of *error*. In that case, too, it is not a new trial, but the same trial continued; though it is often called, improperly, a new trial.*

³ It is the custom in most countries to make accused persons testify against themselves, and, formerly, when the accused did not answer the questions as the judge wished him to do, he could be tortured until he confessed all that he had done, and a great deal that he had not done. This injustice is prevented by this section. An accused person may plead guilty, if he chooses, and confess to as much as he wishes to, of the charge against him; but he is not compelled to say anything unless he wishes to.

Under this section, also, a witness cannot be forced to answer any question which would criminate himself.

⁴ For a definition of bail, see the comments on section 6 of this article.

Capital offenses are those which are punishable with

---

*A person charged with crime is not put twice in jeopardy by a new trial, when the jury fails to agree, or when a *nolle prosequi* is entered on an indictment, (Wis. Reports, Vol. iv, p. 400), or when a conviction has been set aside and a new trial granted on his own application. (Wis. Reports, Vol. vii. p. 695). See also from Simmons's Digest, page 124).

death. As no crimes are now punished by death in this state, there are, of course, no capital offenses.*

'The writ of *habeas corpus* is a process by which any person unjustly confined, either by private persons or by public officers, can be set free, if he has a right to be free. Any person unjustly detained may sue out a writ of *habeas corpus* before any judge or court commissioner (VII, 23). The person detained and the person detaining him, are then brought immediately before the judge or court commissioner, the case is heard, and if the person held ought to be free, he is set free at once by the judge or court commissioner.†

In time of war and public danger it is often necessary to arrest persons on suspicion, and hold them until proof of their crimes has been secured. In such cases the legislature must suspend the privilege of the writ of *habeas corpus*, and then the officers of the state can imprison any one they please without being liable to have their prisoners freed by a writ of *habeas corpus*.

---

* " Since the abolition of capital punishment, persons charged with murder are in all cases bailable." (Simmons's Digest, page 197, Wis. Reports, Vol. xix, p. 676).

†"Our Constitution secures to every person within the state the privilege of the writ of 'habeas corpus, and the use of that writ is adapted *to all cases of illegal restraint and confinement.*" (Simmons' Digest, p. 386, Wis. Reports, Vol. iii, p. 157.) "Probable cause must be shown before a writ of habeas corpus will be granted; and when it appears *prima facie* from the application itself that there is no sufficient ground for the discharge of the person on whose behalf it is made, the writ will not be granted." (Simmons' Digest, p. 386, Wis. Reports, Vol. xv, p. 479, Vol. xvi, p. 623.)

"A discharge upon habeas corpus is no bar to subsequent proceedings for the same offense." (Simmons' Digest, p. 387, Wis. Reports, Vol. iii, p. 145.)

But "after a person has been discharged on habeas corpus, by a valid order of a court or magistrate having jurisdiction of the writ, a warrant for the same cause, that is, *upon the same warrant,* is unlawful." (Simmons' Digest, p. 387, Wis. Reports, Vol. iv, p. 163.)

SECTION IX.

[1]Every person is entitled to a certain remedy in the laws, for all injuries or wrongs he may receive in person, property, or character, [2]he ought to obtain justice freely, and without being obliged to purchase it, completely and without denial, promptly and without delay, conformably to the laws.

[1]This is a statement of a truth which is only so much talk, except as it is carried out in the laws. This section has no more binding force than any other good advice has. But our statute books show that the legislature has tried to carry this out in good faith. There are very few wrongs to person, property or character, for which redress cannot be had under the laws of Wisconsin.

[2]Every person in the state can " obtain justice freely' and without being obliged to purchase it." Any judge who should take a bribe would be removed from his office by impeachment (VII., 1) or by address (VII., 13), and be fined and imprisoned beside. It costs nothing to prosecute for any crime. The state carries on all criminal suits in its own name and at its own cost; for they are " against the peace and dignity of the state of Wisconsin." (VII., 17.) In civil suits, which are car‑ ried on for the benefit of private persons, each one must pay his lawyer, if he has any, and the party who loses must pay the costs of the suit. With these excep‑ tions, justice costs nothing in Wisconsin.

SECTION X.

[1]Treason against the state shall only consist in levying war against the same, or in adhering to its enemies, giving them aid or comfort. [2]No person shall be convicted of treason unless on the testimony of two witnesses to the same overt act, or on con fession in open court.*

*This is taken directly from the United States constitution (Art. III, sect. 3), putting the state in place of the United States.

'Under this section, any one may talk treason as much as he pleases, and may even conspire against the government, without being punished. Only open acts of war are counted treason.

'Two witnesses are required, because in times of civil war and rebellion party spirit runs so high that one witness might easily swear falsely, or exaggerato the truth.

The confession must be in open court, so that it shall be the real confession of the accused, as he wishes to make it, and so that it shall be truly reported. Confessions of persons accused of any crime are never taken as proof of their guilt, except they are made in open court.

SECTION XI.

The right of the people to be secure in their persons, houses, papers and effects, against unreasonable searches and seizures, shall not be violated, and no warrant shall issue but upon probable cause, supported by oath or affirmation, and particularly describing the place to be searched, and the persons or things to be seized.*

Under this section, the officers of the law cannot search any house and any place they please, to find stolen property. Some one must first swear out a search warrant, and show some reason to think the things wanted are there; and then the person or place can be legally searched—and not before.

*This is copied from the United States Constitution, (Amendment IV,) with a slight change in the last line.

SECTION XII.

No [1]bill of attainder, [2]*ex post facto* law, [3]nor any law impairing the obligation of contracts, shall ever be passed; [4]and no conviction shall work corruption of blood or forfeiture of estate.*

[1]A bill of attainder is a bill to punish a single person or a number of persons, named in the bill, without a regular trial. This was a very common thing in early English history, especially for political crimes. It would have been, for instance, a bill of attainder if Congress, after our civil war, had passed a bill against Jeff. Davis for treason, and sentenced him to death without jury trial before a regular court. Such a thing is forbidden by this clause.†

[2]An *ex post facto* law is one to punish, not only those who may afterward break it, but those who have already, before the law takes effect, done anything contrary to it; or a law which adds a new punishment to former crimes. The Supreme Court has decided that this section of the United States Constitution does not forbid all retrospective laws, but only in criminal cases. "An *ex post facto* law is one which renders an act punishable in a manner in which it was not punishable when it was committed."‡

*The three things forbidden in the first half of this section are forbidden to every state by the United States constitution (Art. I, sect. 10), and are, therefore, forbidden in this state by double authority — that of the state constitution and that of the United States constitution.

†Story, in his work on the United States constitution (section 1344) says: " Bills of attainder, as they are technically called, are such special acts of the legislature as inflict capital punishment upon persons supposed to be guilty of high offenses, such as treason and felony, without any conviction in the ordinary course of judicial proceedings. If an act inflicts a milder degree of punishment than death, it is called a bill of pains and penalties. But in the sense of the constitution, it seems that bills of attainder include bills of pains and penalties," (quoting a decision of the Supreme Court of the United States).
This definition differs from that given in Webster's Dictionary. Judge Story is generally considered better authority on a point of law than J. C. Perkins, who furnished the legal definitions for the last edition of Webster's Unabridged, and Story's definition is, therefore, followed here.

‡ Fletcher vs. Peck, 6 Cranch, 138, quoted in Story, §1344.

For instance, a law to punish with death all murderers who may be convicted of murders they have already done, would be *ex post facto*, because the punishment for that crime is now imprisonment in the state's prison. But a law to hang all persons who are convicted of murder, done after the law goes into effect, would be perfectly constitutional.

'Contracts once made cannot be broken, unless the persons who make the contract all agree to break it. But the law can determine what shall be the conditions of a valid contract. For instance, a contract which is for an immoral purpose, or which involves an immoral consideration, is never valid, and may always be broken. A contract to sell counterfeit money, a contract to kill another person for so much money, a bargain made by a judge to give a wrong decision, would none of them be binding contracts. The parties had no right to make them in the first place, and therefore can break them when they please. The obligation of these contracts is not impaired by the law annulling them; for they never had any obligation. The law can at any time fix the conditions of all future contracts, but it cannot impair the obligation of past contracts, provided, they were legal when they were made. This provision of the constitution in civil cases, is like the proviso against *ex post facto* laws in criminal cases.

'Corruption of blood is punishing children for the sins of their fathers. Under the English common law, when anyone was convicted of treason, he forfeited all his property to the state, and his blood was considered corrupt; so that his children and other relatives could not inherit from him. His link in the chain of inheritance was broken, so that none could inherit property or titles or civil rights from him. This great injustice of punishing children for what their fathers have done, is abolished by this section.

SECTION XIII.

The property of no person shall be taken for public use without just compensation therefor.*

The state has the right of eminent domain, and can take private property for public use whenever it chooses. This section provides that when private property is so taken there shall always be just compensation given for it.†

SECTION XIV.

[1]All lands within the State are declared to be allodial, and [2]feudal tenures are prohibited. Leases and grants of agricultural land, for a longer term than fifeeen years, in which rent or service of any kind shall be reserved, and [3]all fines and like restraints upon alienation, reserved in any grant of land hereafter made, are declared to be void.

[1]*Allodial* lands are those which are held by the owner without being subject to any feudal service or any tax or rent other than the tax levied by the government. Nearly all the land in the United States is allodial.

[2]*Feudal tenure* originally was military service — later, it came to mean any service or rent that is to be perpetual.

---

*Private property cannot be taken for *private* use, without the consent of the owner, even with compensation. Public roads may be opened through any one's land. but private ones cannot, except by consent of the owner. See the decision of the supreme court on this point (Wis. Reports, Vol. xxiv, p. 89.)

† "Where private property is taken for public use, the 'just compensation therefor' which the constitution requires, consists in paying the owner not only the value of the portion taken, but also the diminution of the value of that from which it is severed." (Wis. Reports, vol. xxvii, p. 478.) This was a case of a railroad company cutting up a man's farm. The company was obliged to pay for the damage done to the land, as well as for the land actually used in constructing the railroad; and the rise in the value of other land owned by the plaintiff in consequence of the railroad being constructed, was not allowed as a set-off.

See comments on section I of this article.

The time is limited for which farming land may be rented, because, otherwise, this section might have been evaded by leasing land for a very long period (for instance, for 999 years, the term for which land has sometimes been leased in England). This section is restricted to agricultural lands, because land is frequently leased for building purposes for a longer time than fifteen years.

'Fines and like restraints upon alienation are commonly called " entails," and are frequently used in England to keep large estates together after the death of the owner.

The object of this section is to prevent the growth of a landed aristocracy, such as is the curse of England, to-day. To do this, feudal tenures and entails are both prohibited by this section. *Primogeniture*, or the right of the eldest son to inherit all the real estate with the title, has never been established in this country, and, probably, never will be. These three things, feudal tenures, entails, and primogeniture, are the three pillars of the English aristocracy.

What we want in this country is, that the people who till the land, should own the land; and that anybody who wants land, may be able to get it by offering a fair price for it. The farmers in moderate circumstances, who work their farms themselves, are the backbone of any country. With them, Rome conquered the world; for lack of them, in later years, she lost it again. The honest yeomanry of England were her strength in former days; the lack of that class now is her greatest weakness. Slavery prevented the growth of such a class of independent farmers in the Southern States, and made

c

labor dishonorable, and was, therefore, the cause of the ignorance and poverty of a large part of the whites, as well as of the blacks. If we would be a nation of intelligent freemen, we must never allow the farming class to be divided into a haughty aristocracy and a degraded peasantry. That danger this section helps to guard against.

SECTION XV.

No distinction shall ever be made by law between resident aliens and citizens, in reference to the possession, enjoyment, or descent of property.

Aliens are foreigners who have not yet been naturalized. *Resident aliens* are such foreigners as live in the state. Only aliens needed to be thus protected by the state constitution, for citizens of other states living here are already guaranteed all the rights of citizens of this state by the United States Constitution, (Art. IV., Sect. 2). Non-resident aliens are not protected in the holding of property by either constitution. No distinction has, however, been made against them by law, and it is not likely that there ever will be. Anybody, citizen or foreigner, resident or non-resident, can hold property in this state, under the same conditions.

SECTION XVI.

No person shall be imprisoned for debt arising out of, or founded on a contract, expressed or implied.

No person can be imprisoned for debt in this state, unless he has committed some fraud in regard to it. If he obtained property under false pretenses, he can be imprisoned ; not for the debt, but for the fraud. For the debt, he must be sued in the ordinary way. So, if any one embezzles trust funds, whether he be a public officer, or a guardian, or a trustee of any corporation, he cannot be imprisoned for the debt, but may be for the embezzlement.*

SECTION XVII.

The privilege of the debtor to enjoy the necessary comforts of life shall be recognized by wholesome laws, exempting a reasonable amount of property from seizure or sale for the payment of any debt or liability hereafter contracted.

Under this section the legislature has passed very liberal exemption laws. These laws exempt a homestead of forty acres of land, or a village or city lot, with the building on it, provisions for a year for the family, the necessary tools for a mechanic, the library of a professional man, and a great variety of things, too numerous to mention.

SECTION XVIII.

[1]The right of every man to worship Almighty God according to the dictates of his own conscience shall never be infringed, nor shall any man be compelled to attend, erect, or support any place of worship, or to maintain any ministry, against his consent. [2]Nor shall any control of or interference with the rights of conscience be permitted, or any preference be given by law to any religious establishments or mode of worship. [3]Nor shall any money be drawn from the treasury for the benefit of religious societies, or religious or theological seminaries.

[1]One of the greatest evils of every European country is prevented by this section.

*" The constitutional prohibition of imprisonment for debt extends only to cases of debt arising out of contract, expressed or implied, and does not apply to judgments in actions of ejectment, or other actions, *ex delicto.*" (Wis. Reports, Vol. X, p. 495.) " It does not include damages for those *wrongful* acts which either party to a contract may possibly do, and which, though remotely connected with the contract, were not anticipated by the parties at the time of making it; such as the conversion of personal property by a party in whose hands it has been placed as security for a debt." (Wis. Reports, Vol. XII, p. 52.) " Or the conversion by an attorney of money collected by him for his client." (Wis. Reports, Vol. XIV. p. 226.) The above abstracts of decisions are quoted from Simmons' Digest, p. 405.

There is complete religious freedom here. Any one may believe and teach whatever he pleases, so long as he does not do anything that interferes with other people's rights. Any one may believe and teach the doctrine of the Thugs of India; that it is pleasing to their goddess to have them rob and murder travelers. We should have a right to think and to say that it is a very wicked religion; but we could not punish any one by law for believing and teaching it. But let one try to put it in practice by actually robbing and murdering some one, and he can be arrested, tried and punished; not for his wicked belief, but for his wicked actions. So, the Mormons may believe in polygamy, and preach it in this state, without any legal punishment. But if one of them should try to put his belief in practice in this state, by marrying two or three wives, he would be punished; not as a Mormon, but as a bigamist.

² Under this section, no particular form of religion can be taught in our public schools; for that would be preference given by law to some mode of worship; and, therefore, the constitution wisely provides that our common schools shall be unsectarian. (X. 3.)

³ The last sentence of the section would, unless repealed, stop the project proposed by several bodies of Christians, of dividing the school money among the different denominations, for sectarian schools to take the place of our common schools.

SECTION XIX.

No religious tests shall ever be required as a qualification for any office of public trust, under the State, and no person shall be rendered incompetent to give evidence in any court of law or equity, in consequence of his opinions on the subject of religion.

Religious tests have been a great evil in Europe. They are prohibited here. Any person who is otherwise qualified, may hold any office in the state, no matter what his religious opinions may be. And no person can be prevented from testifying in any court, because of his religious opinions. If the members of certain religious bodies were not allowed to testify, it would be as much as to say, that they could not be believed under oath; which would be an unjust stigma to fix on any form of religious faith; for there are honest men in all.

SECTION XX.

The military shall be in strict subordination to the civil power.

We wish to guard against a military despotism in this country. We do not wish to have a successful general seize the government with the help of his army; and we do not intend ever to give him a chance to do it.

The militia of this state is under the command of the Governor, who is commander in chief; and is raised or disbanded at the pleasure of the legislature. Soldiers are responsible to their officers, they to their superiors, and they to the Governor, as commander-in-chief. Should he misuse his office, he can be impeached and removed; so that by this means, the military is subordinate to the civil power.

SECTION XXI.

Writs of error shall never be prohibited by law.

After any criminal case or civil suit has been decided, if the decision is wrong by reason of any informality in the proceedings, or a wrong decision in regard to the law, it can be corrected by a " writ of error," which carries it up to a higher court, where, if the decision is wrong, a new trial will be ordered. *

SECTION XXII.

The blessings of a free government can only be maintained by a firm adherence to justice, moderation, temperance, frugality and virtue, and by frequent recurrence to fundamental principles.

Of course, this has no binding force. It is only a recommendation, which the people can follow or not as they please. We cannot make people good by law. We can only stop them from doing anything very bad; but though we cannot make people virtuous by law, we need to have them so, to have the laws amount to anything. In this country the people make the men who make the laws, and the men who enforce the laws. Our free government depends upon the people, who can make it a blessing or a curse, according as they are themselves intelligent, upright and virtuous, or the opposite. It will do no good to write this constitution on paper, unless the people of Wisconsin are themselves, as expressed in this twenty-second section, just, moderate, temperate, frugal and virtuous; and unless they know the principles on which our government is founded. That they may know these principles, the legislature has wisely decided that this constitution shall be taught in our common schools; and it ought to be taught so that the scholars shall not only know the words, but so that they shall understand its principles, and know the reasons for them.†

*" The constitutional provision that writs of error shall never be prohibited, was not intended to prevent any limitation of that right. Chapter 61, laws of 1858, which limits the time for bringing the writ to two years, is valid. " (Simmons' Digest, page 259. Wis. Reports, vol. xii, p. 371.)

† Aristotle said 2,000 years ago: " But whosoever endeavors to establish

ARTICLE II.

BOUNDARIES.

Articles II and IX logically belong together, as both treat of the jurisdiction of the state. The subject of the jurisdiction of the state comes naturally before that of the forms and powers of the state government, of which the articles that follow treat, because we first wish to know *what* is to be governed, before we know *how* it is to be governed. The analysis of articles II and IX is, therefore, given in this place, and given as if they were one article, as they might better have been. But the text and comments upon article IX are given in their place under that article :

JURISDICTION OF THE STATE.	1. *Boundaries,*	- - - Article II. Section 1	
	2. *Restrictions on State juris-diction,*	1. No interference with United States titles, 2. No tax on United States land, 3. No unequal tax on any non-resident owners.	2
	Extent of juris-diction,	Article IX. Section 1. Concurrent on lakes and rivers that bound the state, 2. All streams free highways.	1
		3. State succeeds to the property of the Territory of Wisconsin.	2
		4. State has the right of eminent domain,	3

SECTION I.

[1]It is hereby ordained and declared that the State of Wisconsin doth consent and accept of the boundaries prescribed in the act of Congress entitled " an act to enable the people of Wisconsin Territory to form a Constitution and State Government, and for the admission of such State into the Union;" approved August

---

wholesome laws in a state, attends to the virtues and vices of each individual who composes it: and hence it is evident that the first care of a man who would found a state, truly deserving that name, and not nominally so, must be to have his citizens virtuous; for, otherwise, it is merely an alliance for mutual defense."

sixth, one thousand eight hundred and forty-six, to-wit: [2]beginning at the north-east corner of the State of Illinois, that is to say, at a point in the center of lake Michigan where the line of forty-two degrees and thirty minutes of north latitude crosses the same; thence, running with the boundary of the State of Michigan, through lake Michigan, Green Bay, to the mouth of the Menomonee river; thence up the channel of the said river to the Brule river; thence up said last mentioned river to lake Brule; thence along the southern shore of lake Brule, in a direct line to the center of the channel between Middle and South Islands, in the lake of the Desert; thence in a direct line to the head waters of the Montreal river, as marked upon the survey made by Captain Cram; thence down the main channel of the Montreal river to the middle of lake Superior; thence through the center of lake Superior to the mouth of the St. Louis river; thence up the main channel of said river to the first rapids in the same, above the Indian village, according to Nicollett's map; thence due south to the main branch of the river St. Croix; thence down the main channel of said river to the Mississippi; thence down the center of the main channel of that river to the northwest corner of the State of Illinois; thence due east with the northern boundary of the State of Illinois, to the place of beginning, as established by " an act to enable the people of the Illinois Territory to form a Constitution and State Government, and for the admission of such State into the Union on an equal footing with the original States," approved April 18th, 1818.*

[1]These are now the boundaries of the State of Wisconsin. It is not likely that they ever will be changed; for, in order to change them, it is not enough for us to wish them changed; congress must also consent to the change, and so must the legislature of the other state or states concerned. For instance, if we should wish to have that part of Michigan that lies between lake Su-

*The following alteration of the boundary was proposed to Congress at the time this constitution was adopted, but as Congress did not consent to the change, it could not be made; and the words that follow in brackets are not a part of the State Constitution. They are, however, usually given in the published copies of the constitution, and they are, therefore, given here as a matter of history: [*Provided, however,* That the following alteration of the aforesaid boundary be, and hereby is, proposed to the Congress of the United States as the preference of the State of Wisconsin, and if the same shall be assented and agreed to by the Congress of the United States, then the same shall be and forever remain obligatory on the State of Wisconsin, viz: leaving the aforesaid boundary line at the foot of the rapids of the St. Louis river; thence in a direct line bearing southwesterly, to the mouth of the Iskodewabo or Rum river. where the same empties into the Mississippi river; thence, down the main channel of the said Mississippi river, as prescribed in the aforesaid boundary.]

perior and lake Michigan, annexed to this state, we must get the consent of the legislature of Michigan, and of congress, as well as of our own legislature. Should any such change be made, it would be, really, an amendment to this section; but it would not need to be formally amended in any of the ways prescribed by Article XII. Under the United States Constitution (IV., 3,) the consent of the legislatures of the states concerned, and of congress, is enough. That would of itself amend this section without any further action by the State of Wisconsin.

[2]The boundary of Wisconsin is commonly given in the geographies as lake Superior and the State of Michigan on the north, and Michigan and lake Michigan on the east, and sometimes, also, the Mississippi river is given as part of the western boundary. These boundaries are not the true ones. The State of Wisconsin extends to the center of lakes Michigan and Superior; and to the center of the main channel of the Mississippi river. As the states of Wisconsin and Michigan meet in the center of lake Michigan, it is not lake Michigan that bounds Wisconsin on the east, but the State of Michigan, and so on. The correct boundary of Wisconsin in general terms, is as follows: Wisconsin is bounded north by Minnesota and Michigan, east by Michigan, south by Illinois, and west by Iowa and Minnesota.

SECTION II.

[1]The propositions contained in the act of Congress are hereby accepted, ratified and confirmed, and shall remain irrevocable without the consent of the United States; and it is hereby ordained that this state 'shall never interfere with the primary disposition of the soil within the same, by the United States, nor

with any regulations Congress may find necessary for securing the title in such soil to *bona fide* purchasers thereof; [3]and no tax shall be imposed on land the property of the United States; [4]and in no case shall non-resident proprietors be taxed higher than residents. [5]*Provided,* That nothing in this Constitution, or in the act of Congress aforesaid, shall in any manner affect the right of the State of Wisconsin to five hundred thousand acres of land granted to said state, and to be hereafter selected and located, by and under the act of Congress, entitled " an act to appropriate the proceeds of sales of the public lands, and grant pre-emption rights," approved September fourth --- thousand eight hundred and forty-one.

[1] This section can be amended in either of the ways prescribed in Article XII, if the consent of congress is also obtained.

[2] The title to land is of great importance, and in all civilized countries, great pains are taken to make the titles to land secure. The United States has sold, or is still offering for sale, the greater part of the land in the state. Its patents for land are really warranty deeds. The United States guarantees to the purchaser a clear title to the lands. Now, to avoid all trouble, and to make the title perfectly sure, congress provides that the state shall never interfere with titles to land derived from the United States. Otherwise, it is possible that the state might at some future time have claimed, that when the United States ceded the territory to the new State of Wisconsin, they ceded also the right to dispose of those titles. This is now forbidden by the law of congress and by this section of our Constitution. It is a fact, however, that our legislature, like those of several other states, has tried to regulate the United States surveys, and correct the errors in them. These laws were, of course, unconstitutional, and have now been repealed.

The titles to land in the state of Wisconsin all either come from the United States or are endorsed by the United States. The Indians were the original owners of the soil. But when America was discovered by Europeans, they held the Indians' ownership of little account. As between themselves they finally determined that the nation which first discovered a tract of country should have the title to it, provided that the discovery was followed up by occupancy within some reasonable time. European nations had already recognized the fact that a title to land may be acquired by conquest in war, or by peaceful purchase. So that various nations gained title to land in America in some one or other of these three ways:

1. Discovery, followed by occupation;
2. Conquest;
3. Purchase, or vo'untary cession.

It would be interesting to trace out the different nations in which the sovereign power over some part of the United States has been at some time vested, and the various processes by which the sovereign power, and with it the original title to land, and the right of eminent domain, has passed from one nation to another. But we can only take up now our own state.

The original title to land in Wisconsin belonged, of course, to the Indians, so far as savages can be said to have a title to land they do not use to any valuable purpose. This title was, however, disregarded by France, which claimed under the discoveries of Marquette and Joliet, and the settlements made soon after in various parts of the state. In the great war known in American history as the Old French War, France was beaten,

and paid the costs of the war by ceding all her posses-
sions in America to England. This included what is
now Wisconsin. After the Revolutionary War, England in like manner ceded what is now Wisconsin,
to the new nation which had conquered its freedom.
When the United States admitted Wisconsin to the
Union, she was admitted as a sovereign state; and the
United States gave to Wisconsin by the act admitting
her to the Union, the sovereign title to the land, with
certain restrictions, which are embodied in this section
of our constitution. Without counting the Indians, the
territory embraced in what is now the state of Wisconsin, has passed through the following hands:

1. France, by discovery and settlement;
2. England, by conquest;
3. The United States, by conquest;
4. The state of Wisconsin, by peaceable cession.

Now, at every change of sovereignty, the rights of
private owners of land have been carefully guarded.

There was no private ownership among the Indians.

A few patents for land were issued by the French
government, and the rights of owners under them were
guaranteed by the treaty of cession from France to
England. A like guarantee was made in the treaty of
cession from England to the United States, and a like
guarantee is given in the act of congress admitting Wisconsin to the Union, and confirmed by the clause in this
section, forbidding interference with United States titles
to land.

The original title to all the land in Wisconsin thus
depends upon the guarantee of the United States.
Every person who owns a foot of land in Wisconsin

obtained it either from the state or United States or from some person or series of persons, the first of whom received it from the state, the United States, England or France. It is therefore the interest of every person who owns land to defend the government which guarantees him possession of it.

[3] Of course it would not be fair to tax the land that belongs to the United States; for the government is holding it for the general good, and not to make any profit out of it. Therefore congress provided, and the state agreed that the United States land should never be taxed.

[4] The clause that prevents the state from taxing non-resident proprietors higher than residents is put in because that would be a way of interfering with the title to property. The state could easily, were it not for this clause, tax non-resident proprietors so high that they would sell out cheap, or let their land be sold for taxes.

[5] For more about the five hundred thousand acres of land, see art. X, sec. 2. This land was given to the state by the United States, for the benefit of common schools, and the proceeds of its sale form a large part of the school fund of the state.

ARTICLE III.

SUFFRAGE.

Sec.

QUALIFICATIONS OF VOTERS,
1. Male,
2. Twenty-one years old,
3. One year a resident,
4. Must be either
   - a. White citizen,
   - b. White foreigner who has declared his intention,
   - c. Indian made citizen by Congress,
   - d. Civilized Indian; or,
   - e. Negro citizen [by statute],

    1

CLASSES SPECIALLY DISQUALIFIED,
1. Idiots and insane persons,   2
2. Convicts, *unless restored to civil rights*,   2
3. U. S. soldiers and sailors stationed here,   5
4. But *not* persons absent on State or U.S. business,   4
5. Those who have bet on any election are disqualified for that election,   6
6. Duellists,   XIII, 2

MANNER OF VOTING,   3

The following additional restrictions upon suffrage, in regard to the eligibibility of the candidate for office and the time of elections are added to the analysis of this article, to complete the subject:

ELIGIBILITY,
- Judges must be { Voters, Citizens of the U. S., Twenty-five years old, } VII, 10
- Governor and Lieutenant Governor must be { Voters, Citizens of U. S., } V, 2
- Senators and Assemblymen must be { Voters, Residents of their districts, } IV, 6
- State officers must be voters,*   VI, 1
- County, town and district officers must be voters,*   VI, 4
- Ineligible, { Sheriffs (for re-election,) VI, 4; Members of Congress, U. S. Officers, Officers of foreign powers, Criminals, Defaulters, } XIII, 3

TIME OF VOTING,
- At general election, { For Assemblymen and Senators, IV, 4; For Governor and Lieutenant Governor, V, 3; For State officers, VI, 1; For county officers (by law) XIII, 9 }
- At spring election, { For town, village and city officers (by law), XIII, 9; For judges, VII, 9 }

---

* The Constitution does not state the qualifications of the administrative officers of the state, and of county officers. The supreme court has decided that in such cases it is to be presumed that any voter could be elected to these offices.

SECTION I.

[1]Every male person of the age of twenty-one years or upwards, belonging to either of the following classes, [2] who shall have re sided in the state for one year next preceding any election, shall be deemed a qualified elector at such election:

1. White [3]citizens of the United States,
2. White persons of foreign birth, [4]who shall have declared their intention to become citizens, conformably to the laws of the United States on the subject of naturalization,
3. Persons of Indian blood, [5]who have once been declared by law of congress to be citizens of the United States, any subsequent law of congress to the contrary notwithstanding,
4. Civilized persons [6]of Indian descent, not members of any tribe;

Provided, [7]That the legislature, may at any time, extend by law the right of suffrage to persons not herein enumerated; but no such law shall be in force until the same shall have been submitted to a vote of the people at a general election, and approved by a majority of all the votes cast at such election.

[1]It may be asked, if the people rule, why then do they not make the laws directly. The answer is: the people of Wisconsin cannot all leave their business and travel, some of them a long way, so as to get together in one place and make the laws. Even if they could do this, there would be too many of them to do the business of making laws, in any orderly way. And even if they made the laws, they would have to choose somebody to see that the laws were obeyed. It is impossible for the people all to get together in mass meeting and vote what they want done, and then do it. They must choose some one to make laws for them, and to execute those laws; that is to *represent* the people.

The first process of representation is, that the men over 21 years of age, *represent* the women and children and vote for them. Then the men vote for officers to represent them. These officers, as the representatives of the people, make the laws and see that they are obeyed.

The form of every law, as prescribed by Article IV, Section 17, is: " The people of the state of Wisconsin, *represented* in senate and assembly, do enact as follows:" Our government is a representative government. It is not a pure democracy, nor, from the nature of the case, can it be.

²One year's residence is required of voters, so that they shall have time to get acquainted with the politics of our state, and know what they are voting for. Another reason is, so that men shall not come over from some other state, just long enough to say they live here, and vote; and then go back again.

³Any person is a citizen of the United States, who is born in this country, or has been naturalized here, and does not become a citizen of some other nation afterward.* A child born to a foreign ambassador, or to any foreigner living here for a short time only would not be considered a citizen, unless he chose so to be. So, also, the children of our ambassadors, and other citizens who live in foreign countries for a time, would be citizens of the United States, notwithstanding the fact that they were born abroad. Women and children are citizens as well as men. Negroes are citizens as well as white people. But uncivilized Indians are not citizens; because they are not governed by our laws, nor protected by our flag as negroes are, and as women and children are. A citizen of the United States is always a citizen of any state he or she may live in.

⁴If a person who is not a citizen wishes to become one, he must first " declare his intention " before the clerk of the circuit court, or of a United States district court.

*See amendment XIV to the United States constitution.

This he can do at any time. When he has lived five years in this country, he can be naturalized, that is, made a citizen, provided he has " delared his intention " at least two years before. When a man who has a family is naturalized, that makes his wife and all his children who are less than twenty-one years old, also citizens. A woman can also become a citizen in the same way a man can; but that does not give her the right to vote.*

'The third clause about Indians, who have once been declared by law to be citizens, was meant to apply to the Stockbridge Indians, who were all at one time partly civilized, and were therefore made citizens by act of congress. A part of them afterwards wished to go_ back to their savage state again, and be governed by their old tribal customs, instead of by the state laws; and an act of congress was passed to that effect. When this constitution was framed, this clause was inserted, so that these Stockbridge Indians could vote, just as if they were civilized.

'There are quite a number of civilized Indians in this state, who dress and live like white people. They

---

* " Each state being sovereign, except as to matters referred to the general government, may, as an undoubted result of that sovereignty, confer upon aliens all the rights and privileges of citizens of such state: but without compliance with the laws of congress on the subject of naturalization, they cannot become citizens of the United States, within the meaning of the constitution.
" It was the intention of the framers of our state constitution to confer upon aliens, who had declared their intention to become citizens of the United States, the full right of *state citizenship.*" (Simmons' Digest, p. 111; Wis. Reports, Vol. xvi, p. 443.)
But, " a mere declaration of intention to become a citizen, by an alien, father of children of foreign birth, who came with him to this country during their minority, does not make such children citizens of the state or of the United States: and they do not become such until their father becomes fully naturalized, or they themselves comply with the naturalization laws: and therefore *they have no right to vote, and are not liable to military service.*" (Simmons' Digest, p. 112; Wis. Reports, Vol. xvii, p. 585.)

D

are all citizens of the United States, and it is, therefore, fair that they should have the right to vote.

[7] The proviso at the close of this section was specially meant to cover the case of negroes, who could thus have the right to vote given them at any time, by the vote of the legislature and of the people. Accordingly, in 1849, the legislature passed a law to extend the suffrage to negroes. This was voted on at the next election, and was supposed, at that time, to have been lost. Very few people voted on that question at all; and it was thought that the words, "a majority of all the votes cast at such election," meant a majority of all that were cast *for anything.* This majority the law did not have; but it did have a majority of all the votes that were cast *on that subject.* In 1866, the question came before the supreme court, and it was decided that the law needed only a majority of all the votes cast *on that subject,* and that the law was therefore legally passed.[*] Since 1866, therefore, negroes have voted in this state.

Should the question of giving women the right to vote ever come before the people of Wisconsin, they could get that right by a law passed by the legislature, and voted for at the next general election, by a majority of all who vote *on that question.*

SECTION II.

[1]No person under guardianship, *non compos mentis,* or insane, shall be qualified to vote at any election; [2]nor shall any person convicted of treason or felony be qualified to vote at any election unless restored to civil rights.

---

[*] " Sec. 1, Art. 3, of our constitution is to be construed as providing for an extension of suffrage, in case a majority of all the votes *on that subject,* cast at any general election at which the question is submitted, shall be in its favor: and such a majority was sufficient to give effect to § 2, chap. 137, Laws of 1849, extending the right of suffrage to colored persons." (Simmons Digest, p. 247; Wis. Reports, Vol. xx, p. 544.)

[1]A person may be placed under guardianship when it is evident that he cannot take care of himself — either because of continual drunkenness, or idiocy or insanity.

Non compos mentis means " of unsound mind "— an idiot or an insane person.

It is plain that persons who cannot take care of themselves cannot help to govern the state ; and, therefore, ought not to vote.

[2]Felony means, under our law, any state's prison offense. A traitor to our state or nation, of course, ought not to help govern it ; nor should a person who is so bad that he must be sent to state's prison ; therefore, traitors and felons are not allowed to vote. Such persons may be restored to civil rights either by special act of the legislature or by the governor's pardon. It is usual, when convicts have behaved well in prison, to pardon them out a few days before their term is out, so as to restore them thereby to civil rights ; for a pardon puts a convict back, in the eyes of the law, where he was before his offense (V. 6).

SECTION III.

All votes shall be given by ballot, except for such township officers as may by law be directed or allowed to be otherwise chosen.

All votes are now given by ballot, except for overseers of highways.

SECTION IV.

No person shall be deemed to have lost his residence in this state by reason of his absence on business of the United States, or of this state.

If it were not for this proviso in the constitution, a United States ambassador or consul, or a soldier, or a sailor, would lose his residence in this state while he was absent on United States business, and would have to live a year in the state when he came back, before he could vote.   Under this section, every year, many United States officers come back from Washington or elsewhere to vote.   During our civil war, a great many persons were absent from the state on business of the United States in the army, and they could not be spared to come home and vote; and so a law was passed to give the soldiers a chance to vote without coming home. Voting places were established in every Wisconsin regiment and battery, and the soldiers' votes were sent to Madison and counted with the rest.*   Usually, however, persons absent from the state on public business must come home if they wish to vote.   The state cannot set up a voting place wherever two or three persons happen to be, who could vote under this section.

SECTION V.

No soldier, seaman, or marine, in the army or navy of the United States, shall be deemed a resident of this state in consequence of being stationed within the same.

This has the same reason in it as the last section. Soldiers, sailors and marines are citizens, not of the state where they happen to be stationed for the time, but of the state of which they were citizens when they enlisted. If they vote anywhere, they must vote there.   But a soldier or a sailor who has enlisted from this state, and who is stationed here, can vote.

---

*"The act of 1862 authorizing citizen soldiers to vote while out of the state, is valid.   The provision of the constitution (XIII, 5,) that no person shall vote for county officers out of the county in which he resides, does not mean that the voter shall not be allowed to vote for officers of the county in which he resides, when absent therefrom, but that he shall not be permitted to vote for officers of a county in which he does not reside."   [Simmons' Digest, p. 247; Wisconsin Reports, Vol. xvi, p. 398.]

SECTION VI.

[1]Laws may be passed excluding from the right of suffrage all persons who have been or may be convicted of bribery or larceny, or of any infamous crime, [2]and depriving every person who shall make, or become directly or indirectly interested in, any bet or wager depending upon the result of any election, from the right to vote at such election.

[1] A law has been passed which forbids any person convicted of bribery, from voting at any election, unless restored to civil rights.

After the war, a law was also passed forbidding deserters and persons who ran away from the draft, from voting at any election. This law is now repealed, and such persons can now vote.

The constitution also prohibits from voting at any election any inhabitant of the state who is engaged in a duel, either as principal or as accessory. (XIII, 2.)

Duellists may be challenged at the polls, and, if they are proved to be such, they will not be allowed to vote.

It is not necessary, as it is with persons guilty of bribery, that they have been convicted upon a trial before a court.

[2] A law has been passed which excludes any person who is interested in a bet on an election, from voting at that election.

ARTICLE IV.

LEGISLATIVE.

RESTRICTIONS ON LEGISLATION.

The following additional restrictions on the power of the legislature are found in other articles of this constitution:

I. PERSONAL LIBERTY.	1. No bill of attainder,	I, 12
	2. No *ex post facto* law,	I, 12
	3. No law impairing contracts.	I, 12
	4. No corruption of blood or forfeiture of estate,	I, 12
	5. No distinction against resident aliens,	I, 15
	6. No imprisonment for debt,	I, 16
	7. Freedom of conscience,	I, 18
	8. No religious test,	I, 19
II. FEDERAL RELATIONS.	1. No interference with title to land given by United States,	II, 2
	2. No tax on United States land.	II, 2
	3. No unequal tax on non-residents,	II, 2
	4. No toll or duty on navigation,	IX, 1
III. FORM OF SUPREME COURT TO BE CHANGED BUT ONCE,		VII, 4
IV. FINANCIAL.	No loan of credit of the state,	VIII, 3
	No public debt, except { for extraordinary expenses,	VIII, 6
	{ war debt,	VIII, 7
	Mode of voting on financial bills.	VIII, 8
	No debt for internal improvement,	VIII, 10
	No banks without a vote of the people,	XI, 5
V. RELATING TO COUNTIES.	Counties of less than 900 square miles, not to be divided without a vote of the people.	XIII, 7
	No county seat to be removed without a vote of the people,	XIII, 8

SECTION I.

The legislative power shall be vested in a Senate and Assembly.

The legislature of this state, like those of all other states of our Union, is organized after the model of the congress of the United States; with two houses — the upper one, smaller in numbers, and elected for a longer term than the lower house. By this means the lower house will be likely to represent the wishes of the people, and the upper house will be likely to be more cautious in what they do, and oppose any very hasty and inconsiderate action of the lower house.

The legislature has power to pass any laws not forbidden by the state or United States constitution; and it has also power to repeal or amend any laws already passed.*

SECTION II.

The number of the members of the Assembly shall never be less than - fifty-four, nor more than one hundred. The Senate shall consist of a number not more than one-third, nor less than one-fourth, of the number of the members of the Assembly.

The number of members of the first Assembly, called under this constitution, was 66. The number of Senators was then 19. We now have the largest number of both that the constitution allows us, 100 Assemblymen and 33 Senators.

SECTION III.

[1] The legislature shall provide by law for an enumeration of the inhabitants of the state, in the year one thousand eight hundred and fifty-five, and at the end of every ten years thereafter; and at their first session after such enumeration, and also after each enumeration made by the authority of the United States, the legislature shall apportion and district anew the members of the Senate and Assembly, according to the number of inhabitants, [2] excluding Indians not taxed, and soldiers and officers of the United States army and navy.

[1] The United States census is taken every ten years, in the years whose numbers end with zero. The state census is taken every ten years, in the years whose numbers end with five. So that one census or the other is taken every five years. And, therefore, the state is dis-

---

* " The legislature, when not restrained by the federal or state constitutions, may pass whatever laws it deems proper, but it belongs to the judiciary to determine what the law *is* or *has been.* When the legislature undertakes to construe or declare what is the existing law, by means of a declaratory act, it, as a general rule, goes beyond its constitutional sphere, and usurps powers which do not belong to it." (Simmons' Digest, p. 479; ,Chandler's Reports, Vol. ii, p. 212.)

" When the legislature has enacted a law on a given subject, it does not thereupon cease to possess any legislative control over that subject during that session, but on the contrary it may pass other acts at the same session repealing or modifying the first." (Simmons' Digest, p. 479; Wisconsin Reports, Vol. i, p. 513.)

tricted for senators and assemblymen every five years. The reason for having the apportionment twice as often as the apportionment for members of congress, is that the state is being settled so fast that it must be re-districted quite often, or the new parts of the state will not have their fair share of assemblymen and senators.

[2] Indians not taxed are not citizens of the United States, or subject to their jurisdiction, and, therefore, ought not to be represented. United States soldiers and sailors who are not citizens of this state, are not entitled to vote here; (III, 5,) therefore, neither of these class s is counted in apportioning members of the legislature.

SECTION IV.

The members of the Assembly shall be chosen annually by single districts, [1]on the Tuesday succeeding the first Monday in November, [2]by the qualified electors of the several districts; [3]such districts to be bounded by county, precinct, town or ward lines, to consist of contiguous territory, [4]and be in as compact form as practicable.

[1] The day of election is the same day as that of electing congressmen and presidential electors; and also the same day as that of electing all state officers.

[2] The qualified electors of a district are all those who have a right to vote in the state under Art. III. of this constitution, and who reside in the district.

[3] The Assembly districts are to be bounded by county, precinct, town or ward lines, because these are the lines that divide the voting districts. It would make a great deal of confusion and useless trouble if two or three different sets of officers were voted for at the same time and place.

[4] It is provided that the Assembly districts shall be in as compact form as practicable, for the sake of conven-

ience, and also, as far as possible, to prevent the legislature from so arranging the districts as to give an unfair advantage to either political party.

SECTION V.

The senators shall be chosen by single districts of convenient contiguous territory, at the same time and in the same manner as members of the Assembly are required to be chosen, and no Assembly district shall be divided in the formation of a Senate district. The Senate districts shall be numbered in regular series, and the Senators chosen by the odd-numbered districts shall go out of office at the expiration of the first year, and the Senators chosen by the even-numbered districts shall go out of office at the expiration of the second year, and thereafter the Senators shall be chosen for the term of two years.

The senators in the odd-numbered districts are elected in the even years, and the Senators in the even-numbered districts in the odd years.

SECTION VI.

[1] No person shall be eligible to the legislature who shall not have resided one year within the state, and be a qualified elector [2] in the district which he may be chosen to represent.

[1] If a person is a qualified elector, he must have resided one year within the state (III. 1), so that this is superfluous.

[2] Every member of the legislature must be a resident of the district which he is chosen to represent ; so that he shall represent it fairly, as he might not do if he did not live there.

SECTION VII.

[1] Each house shall be the judge of the elections, returns, and qualifications of its own members, [2] and a majority of each shall constitute a quorum to do business; but a smaller number may adjourn from day to day and may compel the attendance of absent members, in such manner and under such penalties as each house may provide.*

* This section is taken, word for word, from the first clause of Art. I, Sec. 5. in the U. S. constitution.

¹ If there is any question as to whether any person elected to either house of the legislature was legally elected, the house to which he claims to belong, must judge of the facts in the case. If he was elected by fraud, or if false returns were made declaring that he had the majority, when he did not really have it; or if he is not legally qualified to be a member of that house, then the Assembly or the Senate, as the case may be, is bound to reject him, and receive the candidate who had the next highest number of votes. But each house is the sole judge of the election and qualifications of its members. If it decides wrongly there is no remedy under the constitution. The election or qualification of a senator or assemblyman cannot be inquired into by the courts under a writ of *quo warranto*, as can that of a state or county officer, (VII. 3).

² A quorum is a sufficient number to do business. The constitution provides that at least half the members of either house must be present before any business can be done; that is, a majority makes a quorum. But if there were no exception to this, it would continually happen that there would be no quorum; because a majority of the members might stay away, either through carelessness or purposely, to prevent any business being done. The constitution, therefore, provides that any number of members may meet and call the roll and adjourn again, so as to keep up the organization; and they may, if necessary, arrest the absent members, and compel them to come in, and thus make a quorum. The sergeant-at-arms, of each house, with his assistants, is always sent to arrest absent members.

Upon the final passage of any financial bill, three-fifths of all the members elected to either house are required to ccnstitute a quorum. (VIII, 8.)

SECTION VIII.

Each house may [1] determine the rules of its own proceedings, [2] punish for contempt and disorderly behavior, [3] and with the concurrence of two-thirds of all the members elected, expel a member; but no member shall be expelled a second time for the same cause.

[1] The rules of each house may be found in any legislative manual. They are very nearly the same as those adopted by other state legislatures and by congress. Many of these rules are adopted by all public meetings, and by societies of every sort. Others of them are only fitted for law-making bodies, and therefore, are only adopted by legislatures and by congress. Together, these rules are called the rules of parliamentary practice, because they gradually grew up in the practice of the English parliament, from which they have been adopted, with slight changes, by every legislative body in the United States.

Under this section, either the Senate or Assembly can alter any of these rules, or make new ones for itself, whenever it chooses. And the rules of the Senate and of the Assembly need not be the same. Each house makes its own rules.

[2] Rules would be of no use unless there was some power to enforce them and to punish for disobedience. Therefore, each house has the right, not only to make the rules of its own proceedings, but to punish those who violate these rules. And this power extends to any one, whether a member of the house or not, who disturbs its proceedings, or who is guilty of what is

called "contempt." This power is the same as that which all courts of law exercise. If any one should refuse to testify before a committee of the legislature, when he is summoned to do so, that would be "contempt." Or if any one, whether a member or not, should insult either house by words or actions done in the presence of the house, or should refuse to obey any proper command of the officers of either house, it would be "contempt." But it would not be considered contempt to say or to write or print anything, however severe, against the legislature, anywhere else. To punish any one for words spoken or published outside the legislature itself, would be to violate the freedom of speech guaranteed by art. I, sect 3, of this constitution. An attempt to bribe a member or to threaten him into supporting or opposing any measure before the legislature, is "contempt." An attempt to arrest a member of the legislature, contrary to section 15 of this article, is " contempt."

The punishments which either house of the legislature can inflict for contempt or disorderly behavior, are reprimand, fine and imprisonment, and for members, expulsion.

' Each house has a right to keep up its moral character and its respectability, by expelling members who are notoriously unworthy. But this power might easily be abused for partizan purposes. Therefore, it is guarded by two provisions: first, to expel a member requires the votes of two-thirds of all the members elected; and, second, if the expelled member should be re-elected, he cannot be expelled a second time for the same offense, as a member of either house of congress may be. (U. S. Const. I, 5)

SECTION, IX.

[1] Each house shall choose its own officers, [2] and the Senate shall choose a temporary President, when the Lieutenant Governor shall not attend as President, or shall act as Governor.

[1] The officers of the Senate are the President, Chief Clerk and Sergeant-at-Arms. The officers of the assembly are the same, except that the presiding officer is called the Speaker. These officers are elected by each house, except the President of the Senate when the Lieutenant Governor fills that place.

[2] The Lieutenant Governor is, by virtue of his office, President of the Senate (V, 8.), but he cannot act as Governor and as Lieutenant Governor at the same time. When he acts as Governor, or in any other way vacates his office, or is absent from the Senate chamber, there must be somebody to act as the presiding officer of the Senate. The Senate, therefore, elects a temporary president from its own members, in such cases, and it has become the practice for the Senate at the beginning of the session to elect a President *pro tempore*, who presides whenever the Lieutenant Governor is absent.

SECTION X.

[1] Each house shall keep a journal of its proceedings, and publish the same, except such parts as require secrecy. The doors of each house shall be kept open, except when the public welfare shall require secrecy. [2] Neither house shall, without the consent of the other, adjourn for more than three days.

[1] Each house must keep a journal of its proceedings, and publish it, for two reasons: first, for convenience; so that it can be referred to when needed, to see what business has been done, and what still remains to be done; and second, for public information. Keeping the

doors of each house open answers the latter purpose also. Any one who chooses can listen to the debates, and, moreover, the reporters of the daily papers make every one who reads their reports virtually a hearer of the debates and votes. By these means, the people watch their representatives.

But it may happen, in case of war or sedition, that the public safety requires secrecy; and there may possibly be some other cases in which it would not be well to have the proceedings made public at once. In such a case an exception may be made to the general rule of publicity, and either house may sit with closed doors, and refuse to publish its proceedings.

² If either house could adjourn when it pleased, for any length of time, one house or the other might stop all business. Like a baulky team, first one and then the other might refuse to pull. But as the members of our legislature are now paid by the year, instead of by the day, it is their interest to finish business as fast as possible, instead of adjourning from day to day, to hinder legislation.

An adjournment for two or three days is frequently made, so that members can go home and stay over Sunday, or over some holiday. But for an adjournment of more than three days a joint resolution, passed by both houses, is necessary.

SECTION XI.

The legislature shall meet at the seat of government, at such time as shall be provided by law, once in each year, and no oftener, unless convened by the Governor.

The time for the meeting of the legislature is the second Wednesday in January. The legislature can not adjourn to meet in special session, as congress can. When it has finished its business, it must adjourn *sine die* (without a day fixed for meeting again); and it can only be called together again by the Governor — and that only on extraordinary occasions. (V. 4.)

SECTION XII.

No member of the legislature shall, during the term for which he was elected, be appointed or elected to any civil office in the state which shall have been created, or the emoluments of which shall have been increased, during the term for which he was elected.

This is taken from the United States constitution (J. 6, clause 2) and has the same reason — to prevent any influential member of the legislature having an office created or made more valuable, and then securing his own appointment or election to that office.

It is only civil office, however, which is thus restricted; for it might easily happen, as it did during our civil war, that the services of some members of the legislature are needed in military offices.

But this restriction does not cover the case of any member of the legislature *after he is elected* to any office having the salary of that office raised. It was an oversight in the framers of both constitutions not to provide against this contingency.

SECTION XIII.

No person being a member of congress, or holding any military or civil office under the United States, shall be eligible to a seat in the legislature; and if any person shall, after his election as a member of the legislature, be elected to congress, or be appointed to any office, civil or military, under the government of the United States his acceptance thereof shall vacate his seat.

This is meant to make the members of the legislature entirely independent of federal influence. They are to represent this state — not the United States. A member of congress, or a federal office-holder, would be likely to be influenced by the United States government. There is a further provision (XIII, 3,) which prohibits any United States officers (except postmasters), or the officers of any foreign power, from holding any office under this state. By comparing these two sections we see that postmasters may hold any office under the state; but cannot be elected to the legislature. Strictly speaking, the members of the legislature are not *officers* of the state, but representatives.

SECTION XIV.

The governor shall issue writs of election to fill such vacancies as may occur in either house of the legislature.

Vacancies in the legislature may occur through death, resignation or expulsion, or acceptance of a seat in congress or a United States office. When a vacancy occurs the governor must set a day for a new election. The person elected on that day holds office for the unexpired term only.

SECTION XV.

Members of the legislature shall, in all cases except treason, felony, and breach of the peace, be privileged from arrest; nor shall they be subject to any civil process, during the session of the legislature, nor for fifteen days next before the commencement and after the termination of each session.

This is a privilege granted to the members of all legislative bodies in this country and in Europe. By the United States constitution (I, 6,) senators and representatives are privileged from arrest in all cases except for treason,

E

felony, or breach of the peace, "during their attendance at the session of their respective houses, and in going to and returning from the same."* Members of the Wisconsin legislature may be arrested for the same crimes as congressmen, at any time and place. But this section of the constitution gives members of the legislature greater privileges. They are privileged from arrest for any other offense than treason, felony or breach of the peace, *during their whole term of office;* and they cannot be sued during the session of the legislature, nor for fifteen days before or after it.

Treason is defined by this constitution (I, 10,) to consist only in levying war against the state, or in adhering to its enemies. Felony is any state's prison offense. Breach of the peace is any act that disturbs public order — such as assault and battery or indecent behavior of any kind.

SECTION XVI.

No member of the legislature shall be liable in any civil action or criminal prosecution whatever, for words spoken in debate.

This is also a privilege given to the members of all legislative bodies everywhere.† There must be complete freedom of speech about measures and about men, in the debates of the legislature, so that the public good shall be best subserved.

---

* The privilege of members of congress from arrest includes also their privilege from any summons or civil process, during the session and in going and returning, though not stated in so many words in the U. S. constitution.

† See U. S. Constitution, I, 6, clause 1.

SECTION XVII.

[1] The style of the laws of the state shall be: "The people of the state of Wisconsin, represented in Senate and Assembly, do enact as follows;" [2] and no law shall be enacted except by bill.

[1] All the laws of Wisconsin begin in these words: "The people of the state of Wisconsin, represented in Senate and Assembly, do enact as follows." The form in which every law must begin, thus shows that the legislature is to represent the people of the state.

[2] The congress of the United States frequently passes joint resolutions of both houses, which have the effect of laws. These must, however, be signed by the president in the same way as bills, (U. S. Const., I, 7). But this is forbidden to the Wisconsin legislature by this section. All laws must be passed in the form of bills; but amendments to the constitution are passed in the form of joint resolutions. So also are memorials to congress. And either house, or both together, may pass any resolutions they choose that only express their opinions, without having the force of laws. Such resolutions, having no legal force, do not need the governor's signature.

SECTION XVIII.

No private or local bill, which may be passed by the legislature, shall embrace more than one subject, and that shall be expressed in the title.

This is to prevent three practices very common in congress and in many state legislatures. The first is that of tacking some private or local bill, which could not pass if attention was called to it, on some other bill to which nobody has any objections, and thus slipping it through the various readings and votes before it is noticed. The second is the practice of combining several private or local schemes in one bill and thus each getting the support of all the members who would support any one of them. The third is the practice of slipping through objectionable measures by an innocent looking title that does not call attention to the main object of the bill.*

The amendment to this article (sections 31 and 32,) stops a great deal of this special legislation, but this section still applies to all local or private bills that are not prohibited by that amendment.

SECTION XIX.

[1] Any bill may originate in either house of the legislature; [2] and a bill passed by one house may be amended by the other.

[1] In congress all bills for raising revenue must originate in the House of Representatives. This restriction is abolished for our state legislature, and bills may originate, that is, be first brought in and passed in either house.

If a bill that passes one house is amended in the other, it is sent back to the house in which it originated, where the amendment is considered. If this house concurs in the amendment, both houses are then agreed on the bill. and it goes to the governor for his signature or veto. But if the first house does not concur in the amendment, a committee of conference is appointed from each house, who meet and try to come to some agreement, until both

---

* " Chapter 269, Private and Local Laws of 1870, which had for its sole object to legalize certain proceedings of the common council of Janesville, but is entitled, " An act to legalize and authorize the assessment of street improvements," is invalid because it does not show the locality to which it applies, and, therefore, does not " express the subject " thereof within the meaning of section 18, article 4, of the state constitution." (Wis. Reports, Vol. xxvi, p. 697.)

houses either agree on something, or find that they cannot agree. In this latter case, of, course, the bill is lost.

SECTION XX.

The yeas and nays of the members of either house, on any question, shall, at the request of one-sixth of those present, be entered on the journal.

This differs from a like provision in the United States constitution (I, 5, clause 3,) in requiring only one-sixth of those present, instead of one-fifth, to call for the yeas and nays. When the yeas and nays are called for, if one-sixth of those present concur in the call, the roll of members is called over by the clerk, and each member who is present answers in his turn, "aye" or "no." The names of those voting on each side of the question are recorded by the clerk in the journal, and published. The yeas and nays are very frequently called for in our legislature, and the result is always published in the leading newspapers, so that any one who chooses to know, can always tell how any member of the legislature voted on any important question.

The yeas and nays *must* be taken in the following cases:

1. In each house, upon the passage of a bill creating a state debt. (VIII, 6.)

2. In each house, upon the passage of any financial measure. (VIII, 8.)

3. In each house, upon the passage of a bill over the governor's veto. (V, 10.)

4. In each house, upon the passage of a proposed amendment to the constitution. (XII, 1.)

In these cases, it is only upon the *final passage* of

these measures that the vote must be taken by yeas and nays, and entered upon the journal.

5. But the yeas and nays may be called for upon any vote that is taken upon any question; and if the call is sustained by one-sixth of those present, the vote *must* be taken by yeas and nays, and entered upon the journal. (IV, 20.)

6. All elections made by the legislature must be made by a *viva voce* vote, which is similar to the vote by yeas and nays, the only difference being that each member announces the name of the candidate for whom he votes, instead of saying " aye " or " no." In both cases the votes are entered upon the journal, (IV, 30.) The only exception to this is in case an election for governor should go to the legislature, in which case the election is by joint ballot. (V, 3.)

SECTION XXI.

[1]Each member of the legislature shall receive for his services three hundred and fifty dollars per annum, and ten cents for every mile he shall travel in going to and returning from the place of meetings of the legislature, [2]on the most usual route. In case of an extra session of the legislature, no additional compensation shall be allowed to any member thereof, either directly or indirectly.*

[1]As the members now receive an annual salary, it is their interest to get through with business as soon as possible, and it is not their interest to have extra sessions.

[2] The mileage is to be calculated upon the most usual route, to prevent members going a long distance out of

*This section was amended November 5, 1867. Before that it was as follows: "Each member of the legislature shall receive for his services, two dollars and fifty cents for each day's attendance during the session, and ten cents for every mile he shall travel in going to and returning from the place of the meeting of the legislature on the most usual route."

their way on business or for pleasure, and getting mileage for that extra travel.

SECTION XXII.

The legislature may confer upon the [1]boards of supervisors of the several counties of the state, [2]such powers, of a local, legislative and administrative character, as they shall from time to time prescribe.

[1] The board of supervisors consists now in each county of the chairmen of the town boards and a supervisor elected by each incorporated village and by each ward of a city. They elect their own chairman, and the county clerk acts as their clerk.

[2] The legislature has given the boards of supervisors a great many powers of a local character, of which only a few of the most important can be here specified:

1. They have charge of all the buildings and other property of the county.

2. They examine and settle all accounts against the county.

3. They fix the salaries of county officers, within the limits prescribed by law.

4. They apportion taxes among the various towns, villages and wards in the county, and they levy all taxes needed to pay the expenses of the county government.

5. They may change the name of any person, town or village in the county.

6. They may change the boundaries of any town or village in the county.

7. They may incorporate literary, benevolent, charitable and scientific institutions.

8. They may grant charters for ferries and plank and turnpike roads, and fix the rates of toll.

SECTION XXIII.

The legislature shall establish but one system of [2]town and [1]county goverment, [3]which shall be as nearly uniform as practicable.

[1]Like the state government, the county government consists of legislative, executive, administrative and judicial officers.

The board of supervisors is the county legislature, with the powers named in he notes to the last section.

The executive officers of a county are sheriff and coroner.

The administrative officers are clerk, treasurer, register of deeds, surveyor, district attorney and school superintendent.

The judicial officers are county judge, clerk of the circuit court and one or more court commissioners The powers and duties of these officers are given elsewhere; those of the executive and administrative officers under Article VI, section 4, and those of the judicial officers under Article VII, sections 12, 14 and 23.

[2]The town government is simpler than either county, state or national. The legislature consists of all the voters in the town, who meet on the first Tuesday in April, hear reports of officers, vote taxes for schools, for roads and bridges, for the poor and for such other town purposes as may be necessary; make such orders and by-laws for governing the town as they think necessary, and elect the following officers by ballot:

1. A town board of supervisors, consisting of three members, who enforce all orders and by-laws of the town, audit all accounts, fill all vacancies in town offices, and act as trustees of the town property. The chairman represents the town in the county board.

2. A town clerk.

3. A town treasurer, who collects taxes and keeps the money of the town subject to the order of the supervisors.

4. An assessor, who takes a list of all the taxable property in the town, with the value of it.

5. Four constables.

6. Four justices of the peace, of whom two are elected every year.

7. Overseers of highways, who need not be elected by ballot unless the voters please to do so.

The town government is almost a pure democracy. The voters of each town assemble and discuss all matters of common concern, and decide them by a majority vote. But it is found to be impossible, even in so small a territory as a single town, for the voters in a body to do all the administrative, executive and judicial business of the town. For this, they have to elect officers; but the voters are themselves the legislature of the town.

ˢThis system of town and county government has been changed several times by the legislature. County superintendents of schools have been substituted for town superintendents. The composition of the county board of supervisors has been twice changed; but these changes have been uniform throughout the state. Whenever the legislature has given one county a system of government in any respect different from the rest, the supreme court has decided the act to be unconstitutional.*

* "An act providing for a county board of *eight* supervisors in a certain county, which under the general statute relative to county government would have only *three*, is in conflict with section 23, article 4, of the state constitution." (Wis. Reports, Vol. xxiv, p. 484.)

"Sec. 23, art. iv, of our state constitution, which provides that the legislature shall establish but one system of town and county government, and that this 'shall be as nearly uniform as possible,' is *mandatory*; and the

SECTION XXIV.

[1] The legislature shall never authorize any lottery, [2] or grant any divorce.

[1] This prohibits all lotteries. The legislature can neither itself legalize a lottery nor give power to any state, county, city, village or town officers to authorize a lottery. What the legislature cannot do itself, it might be constitutional for it to empower some one else to do, as is the case with divorces, which the legislature itself cannot grant, but which it has authorized circuit judges to grant. But in this case, the legislature is not allowed to *authorize* a lottery. To allow anybody else to give power for a lottery, would be just as much an authorizing of lotteries as if the legislature should itself grant licenses to them, only it would be doing it indirectly instead of directly.

Gift enterprises of all sorts have been often decided by the courts to be lotteries, and are therefore contrary to law. .

[2] Divorces are granted by the circuit judges at the regular term of court, for the causes named in the laws. The legislature cannot itself grant any divorce, but it has passed a general law under which divorces can be granted by the courts, for certain specified causes.

SECTION XXV.

The legislature shall provide by law that all stationery required for the use of the state, and all printing authorized and required by them to be done for their use, or for the state, shall be let by contract to the lowest bidder; but the legislature may establish a maximum price. [2] No member of the legislature, or other state officer shall be interested, either directly or indirectly, in any such contract.

court must declare invalid any enactment in violation thereof." (Wis. Reports, Vol. xxx, p. 541.)
The act establishing the office of county auditor, for the county of Milwaukee only, is, therefore, invalid.

¹ This is to prevent any frauds in the state printing. It cannot be given as a reward for party seivices, but must be given to the person who will do the work the cheapest. "A maximum price" means the highest price which will be given. The legislature may say that no more than so much will be paid in any case, to prevent a combination of printers to keep prices up.

² Members of the legislature and state officers are forbidden to have any interest in contracts for state printing, so that there shall be no suspicion of any corrupt bargains, or fraud of any kind.

SECTION XXVI.

The legislature shall never grant any extra compensation to any public officer, agent, servant, or contractor, after the services shall have been rendered or the contract entered into. Nor shall the compensation of any public officer be increased or diminished during his term of office.

This is to make public officers and contractors entirely independent of the legislature. Having nothing to hope or to fear in the way of salary, they will be more likely to do their work faithfully.

SECTION XXVII.

The legislature shall direct by law in what manner and in what court suits may be brought against the state.

It has been provided by law that no person can sue the state for any claim he has against it, until he has presented it to the legislature and they refuse to allow it. He must notify the attorney general, who is the state's lawyer, and who must defend the state in the trial of the case. The case is tried before the supreme court so far as the law of the case is concerned. If the facts have to be proved, the case is sent down to some circuit court where it is tried before a jury, who decide upon the facts, as in any civil suit, and their judgment is sent up to the supreme court, and a verdict rendered in accordance with the facts as decided by the jury, and the law as interpreted by the supreme court.

SECTION XXVIII.

Members of the legislature, and all officers, executive and judicial, except such inferior officers as may be by law exempted, shall, before they enter upon the duties of their respective offices, take and subscribe an oath or affirmation to support the constitution of the Untted States, and the constitution of the state of Wisconsin, and faithfully to discharge the duties of their respective offices to the best of their ability.

The oath is taken unless the officer has conscientious scruples against taking an oath; in that case, he simply affirms instead of swearing.

SECTION XXIX.

The legislature shall determine what persons shall constitute the militia of the state, and may provide for organizing and disciplining the same, in such manner as shall be prescribed by law.

There are several militia laws upon the statute books, but they are not enforced. In theory, all the able-bodied males in the state, between the ages of eighteen and forty-five, who are not specially exempted, belong to the state militia. In actual practice, the state militia consists of the governor's staff and the volunteer companies organized in several of the cities and villages.

A volunteer company may be formed anywhere in the state, where sixty-five persons subject to military duty wish to be organized into a military company. They elect their own officers annually. They are exempt from poll tax and jury duty, and are liable to be called out by the governor and other officers, in case of war, insurrection, riot or resistance to the laws. In case of war, volunteers may be called for, and if enough do not volunteer, a draft may be ordered. The soldiers who then volunteer or are drafted, may serve under the authority of the state, or they may be sworn into the United States service.

SECTION XXX.

[1] In all elections to be made by the legislature, the members thereof shall vote [2] *viva voce*, and their votes shall be entered on the journal.

[1] The legislature elects the United States senators from this state, and each house elects its own officers, except the president of the Senate, when the lieutenant-governor fills that place.

The elective officers of each house are : for the Senate, the president *pro tem.*, chief clerk and sergeant-at-arms; and for the Assembly, the speaker, chief clerk and sergeant-at-arms, (XIII, 6). The other officers are appointed.

[2] *Viva voce* means, literally, " with the living voice." A *viva voce* vote is one in which those who vote, do so with their voice, not by ballot, or by a show of hands, or by rising.

The object of having the vote *viva voce*, and having each vote entered on the journal, is to make it public, and, therefore, as fair as possible.

SECTION XXXI.

(Adopted at the general election, Nov. 7, 1871.)

The legislature is prohibited from enacting any special or private laws in the following cases: 1st. For changing the name of persons, or constituting one person the heir-at-law of another. 2d. For laying out, opening or altering highways except in cases of state roads extending into more than one county, and military roads, to aid in the construction of which lands may be granted by congress. 3d. For authorizing persons to keep ferries across streams, at points wholly within this state. 4th. For authorizing the sale or mortgage of real or personal property of minors or others under disability. 5th. For locating or changing any county seat. 6th. For assessment or collection of taxes, or for extending the time for the collection thereof. 7th. For granting corporate powers or privileges, except to cities. 8th. For authorizing the apportionment of any part of the school fund. 9th. For incorporating any town or village, or to amend the charter thereof.

All these cases can be better provided for each by a general law which will cover all cases that will arise, than they would be by having the legislature pass a special law for every particular case. For instance, it is a great deal better to give the business of changing people's names to the county board or the county judge, and not trouble the legislature with it. The result of special legislation always is to cause corruption and bribery of members and indiscriminate haste in passing laws, and to burden the statute books with a great number of private and local laws. The legislature is made the theater of contending local or private interests, to the exclusion of measures of great public utility, but in which no one is pecuniarily interested. The experience of this and other states has, therefore, shown that the public good will be best promoted by excluding as much special legislation as possible.

In addition to the nine cases named in section 31, the constitution forbids special laws in the following cases:

1. No bill of attainder can be passed; that is, a bill punishing particular persons by name. (I, 12.)

2. No preference can be given by law to any particular religious establishment or mode of worship. (I, 18.)

3. There can be but one system of town and county government. (IV, 23.)

4. The legislature can grant no divorce (IV, 24).

5. The state printing must be given to the lowest bidder (IV, 25).

6. Officers cannot receive extra pay (IV, 26).

7. The rule of taxation must be uniform (VIII, 1).

8. The supreme court has decided that acts of the legislature exempting particular persons or corporations from *any* general law are void.*

SECTION XXXII.

(Adopted at the general election, Nov. 7, 1871.)

The legislature shall provide general laws for the transaction of any business that may be prohibited by section thirty-one of this article, and all such laws shall be uniform in their operation throughout the state.

The legislature has provided general laws for all these cases.

*As a rule, acts of the legislature exempting particular individuals, or corporations by name, from the operation of general laws, are not within the proper scope of the legislative power, and are void. (Wis. Reports, vol. xxx, p. 464.)

ARTICLE V.

EXECUTIVE.

SECTION I.

[1]The executive power shall be vested in a governor who shall hold his office for two years. [2]A lieutenant governor shall be elected at the same time, and for the same term.

[1] The executive power is vested in one man rather than in a committee or board, because experience has shown that one man who has the whole responsibility will be more efficient in carrying out the laws than several together would be. When laws are to be made, it is better

to have them considered by a number of persons, so as to get the wisdom of all. But where laws are to be enforced, it is better to give all the responsibility to one man, so that what is to be done can be done speedily and thoroughly. Wisdom is needed in making the laws, and that is secured by having a large legislature; but energy is needed in carrying out the laws, and that is secured by having a single executive.

² The president holds his office for four years. The governor of Wisconsin holds his office for two years only. He can, however, be re-elected as many times as the people choose to make him governor. No governor has yet served longer than six years.

³ The lieutenant governor is elected like the vice president, for the same term as his chief. This is because he may be called on to take his place.

SECTION II.

¹ No person, except a citizen of the United States and a qualified elector of the state, shall be eligible to the office of ² governor or lieutenant governor.

¹ No person can be president or vice president of the United States who is not a native born citizen. But a foreigner who has been naturalized is eligible to the office of governor or lieutenant governor. A foreigner can vote, after he has been here a year, if he takes out his papers declaring his intention to become a citizen of the United States, but he cannot be elected governor, lieutenant governor, or judge of the circuit or supreme courts until he becomes a citizen.

² The lieutenant governor must have the same qualifications as the governor, because he is frequently made acting governor by reason of the governor's sickness or

F

absence from the state; and he would be made governor should the governor die, resign, or be removed upon an impeachment. He must have the same qualifications as the governor because he may have to take the governor's place.

SECTION III.

[1]The governor and lieutenant governor shall be elected by the qualified electors of the state, at the times and places of choosing members of the legislature. [2]The persons respectively having the highest number of votes for governor and lieutenant governor shall be elected. But in case two or more shall have an equal and the highest number of votes for governor or lieutenant governor, the two houses of the legislature, at its next annual session, shall forthwith, by joint ballot, choose one of the persons so having an equal and the highest number of votes for governor or lieutenant governor. The returns of election for governor and lieutenant governor shall be made in such manner as shall be provided by law.

[1]As the governor and lieutenant governor hold office for two years, it is only every other year that an election for governor and lieutenant governor occurs. This election is in the odd years, while the election for members of congress comes in the even years, and the presidential election comes in the leap years.

[2]In the election of president and vice president, a majority of all the votes cast by the presidential electors is necessary to a choice (U. S. const. Amendment XII), so that if there are three or more candidates, it may very well happen that none of them receives a majority. But the state constitution provides that a plurality shall elect, so that it does not matter how many candidates there may be for the office of governor or lieutenant governor, the person who has the highest number of votes, although that may not be a majority of all, is elected. It is not at all likely, but it is barely

possible, that there may be a tie vote. In that case, should it ever occur, the legislature must decide between the two or more candidates who received an equal and the highest number of votes. This must be done by joint ballot of the two houses of the legislature. In a joint ballot, both houses sit together as if they were one, and each member has one vote. If they do not choose the governor or lieutenant governor on the first ballot, they must keep on balloting until they do elect one or the other of the candidates. This must be the first business of the legislature after organizing. The word "forthwith" in this section requires that.

SECTION IV.

[1] The governor shall be [2] commander-in-chief of the military and naval forces of the state. [3] He shall have the power to convene the legislature on extraordinary occasions; and in case of invasion, or danger from the prevalence of contagious disease at the seat of the government, he may convene them at any other suitable place within the state. [4] He shall communicate to the legislature, at every session, the condition of the state, and recommend such matters to them for their consideration as he may deem expedient. [5] He shall transact all necessary business with the officers of the government, civil and military. [6] He shall expedite all such measures as may be resolved upon by the legislature, and shall take care that the laws be faithfully executed.

[1] This section contains a summary of the powers and duties of the governor, except the power of pardon and the veto power; for which, see sections 6 and 10. An analysis of all the powers and duties of the governor is given at the beginning of this article.

It is well to notice that the governor of Wisconsin does not have some powers which the president has. He has no power to make treaties, because the state of Wisconsin is not an independent nation, and, therefore, cannot make treaties through any branch of its government. For the same reason he does not appoint ambassadors or consuls. He does not appoint the judges or the heads of the state departments ; for these, in Wisconsin, are elected by the people. And his power of granting pardons is limited.

² As the president is commander-in-chief of the militayr and naval forces of the United States, so is the governor commander-in-chief of the military and naval forces of the state of Wisconsin. The state does not yet have any naval forces, although it is possible for it to have ships of war upon lake Michigan and the Mississippi river, if congress should consent to it (U. S. const. I, 10). But the state has no use for a navy ; being protected against foreign enemies by the whole power of the United States.

The military forces of the state consist in time of peace, of the various volunteer companies which are organized under the state military laws. In time of war, the state military forces consist, in addition to the regular militia, of the volunteer and drafted soldiers who are enlisted for that special occasion. These are usually sworn into the service of the United States, and are then no longer under the authority of the governor, but under that of the president. Their officers, however, are appointed by the governor, even while they are in the service of the United States, by virtue of article I, section 8 of the United States' constitution.

³The governor may call a special session of the legislature whenever, for any reason, their action is needed, and cannot be put off until the regular session.

In case of invasion, when the enemy's army has taken or is likely to take the capitol, or when a contagious disease makes the capital a dangerous place, he can call the legislature at either their regular session or a special one, to meet at such other place in the state as he thinks best.

'The governor's message is always sent at the opening of the regular session of the legislature.

The governor gives a brief report of the condition of the state, and sends with it the reports of all the different state officers and official boards. He gives, also, any recommendations that he pleases, which the legislature adopts or not, as it chooses. When he calls a special session, he must, of course, send a message to the legislature to inform them why he called them together, and what it is that he wishes to have them act upon at that special session.

'The governor acts as representative of the state, and as such must transact all necessary business with the officers of the state. He also represents the state in all its business with other states or with the United States, except where some other officer is expressly named to represent the state for certain purposes.

'The governor is the executive of the state, and as such, he must see that the laws are faithfully executed. He has no choice in this matter. Whether he thinks that a law is right or wrong, he must see that it is executed. If force is used to prevent the execution of a law, he can call on the militia and police forces, and if there should be serious resistance to them, he can call on the United States army to help him enforce the laws. (U, S. Const. IV, 4.)

SECTION V.

The governor shall receive during his continuance in office, an annual compensation of five thousand dollars, which shall be in full for all traveling or other expenses incident to his duties.*

The salary of the governor of Wisconsin is five thousand dollars. That of the president of the United States is fifty thousand dollars.

SECTION VI.

[1] The governor shall have power to grant reprieves, commutations, and pardons, after conviction, for all offenses, except treason and cases of impeachment, upon such conditions and with such restrictions and limitations as he may think proper, [2] subject to such regulations as may be provided by law relative to the manner of applying for pardons. [3] Upon conviction for treason, he shall have the power to suspend the execution of the sentence until the case shall be reported to the legislature, at its next meeting, when the legislature shall either pardon, or commute the sentence, direct the execution of the sentence, or grant a further reprieve. He shall annually communicate to the legislature each case of reprieve, commutation of pardon granted, stating the name of the convict, the crime of which he was convicted, the sentence and its date, and the date of the commutation, pardon, or reprieve, with his reasons for granting the same.

[1] A reprieve is a delay in the execution of a sentence, especially a sentence of death. A commutation of a sentence is to change it for one less severe. A pardon is a reversal of the sentence; a pardon stops all further punishment, and restores the criminal to his civil rights. (See III, 2.)

From the nature of the case, the governor must have almost unlimited power to pardon; for no laws made beforehand can cover all the cases that may deserve pardon. Therefore, the governor's power to pardon

---

* This section is given above as it now stands. It was amended by a vote of the people at the general election held Nov. 2, 1869. Previous to that time it read as follows:

"The governor shall receive during his continuance in office, an annual compensation of one thousand two hundred and fifty dollars."

must be discretionary. It is limited, however, in four points:

(1) The legislature prescribes the manner of applying to the governor for a pardon.

(2) In cases of treason, the governor cannot pardon absolutely, but only with the concurrence of the legislature.

(3) In cases of impeachment he cannot pardon at all.

(4) And he must report to the legislature all the pardons he grants, and his reasons for granting them.

² The manner of applying for a pardon is very carefully prescribed by law, so that only those who deserve pardons shall get them.

³ In cases of treason the governor has no power to pardon. He can only suspend the sentence long enough for the legislature to act upon it. The governor may do this or not, as he chooses. But if he does suspend the sentence of a person convicted of treason, the legislature must act upon it in some way.

SECTION VII.

¹In case of the impeachment of the governor, or his removal from office, death, inability from mental or physical disease, resignation, or absence from the state, the powers and duties of the office shall devolve upon the lieutenant governor, for the residue of the term, or until the governor, absent or impeached, shall have returned, or the disability shall cease. ²But when the governor shall, with the consent of the legislature, be out of the state in time of war, at the head of the military force thereof, he shall continue commander-in-chief of the military force of the state.

¹The governor may go out of office, either temporarily or permanently. He goes out of office temporarily in case he is impeached (VII, 1), and permanently, should he, on the impeachment trial, be found guilty by the

senate. He goes out of office temporarily when he is so sick or so out of his right mind that he cannot discharge the duties of his office ; and permanently in case of his death. He goes out of office temporarily whenever he goes out of the state ; and permanently should he ever resign. When he goes out of office temporarily, the lieutenant governor acts as governor as long as he stays out of office ; but when he goes out of office permanently the lieutenant governor becomes governor for the rest of the two years for which they were both elected.

The question is not decided by the United States constitution whether an officer who is impeached is suspended from his office while under trial. When President Johnson was impeached, it was decided that a United States officer who is impeached, is not, therefore, suspended; and the president went on with the duties of his office while he was being tried. The framers of our state constitution provided that whenever the governor is impeached, he shall be suspended from his office during the time of the trial, and the lieutenant governor shall act as governor. Judges who may be impeached are suspended while under trial (VII, 1). The inference is that any other officer who may be impeached will retain his office until he is convicted.

'The exception is made, that whenever in time of war, the governor goes out of the state to command the state troops, he shall still be governor, so far as being commander-in-chief is concerned. But he can only do this with the consent of the legislature; and the lieutenant governor will act as governor in every other respect.

SECTION VIII.

[1]The lieutenant governor shall be president of the senate, but shall have only a casting vote therein. [2]If during a vacancy in the office of governor, the lieutenant governor shall be impeached, displaced, resign, die, or from mental or physical disease become incapable of performing the duties of his office, or be absent from the state, the secretary of state shall act as governor until the vacancy shall be filled, or the disability shall cease.

[1]Just as the vice president is president of the United States senate, so the lieutenant governor is president of the state senate. He has no vote on ordinary occasions, because he is not a member of the senate; but when there is a tie vote, on any question, he has then a casting vote (or deciding vote); not as a member, but as the presiding officer of the senate.

[2]When the lieutenant governor is acting as governor, or if he is sick or absent, or if he should be impeached, or resign, or die, he cannot, of course, preside in the senate. The senate in that case elect one of their own number president *pro tempore* (for the time). The president *pro tempore* has a vote on all questions as a member of the senate, but has no casting vote. But the president of the senate does not act as governor when the governor and lieutenant governor are both incapacitated, as the president of the United States senate does when the president and vice president are both incapacitated. This duty comes on the secretary of state, who is the next highest elective officer of the state.

SECTION IX.

The lieutenant governor shall receive during his continuance in office, an annual compensation of one thousand dollars.*

*This section is given above as it now reads. Before its amendment in 1869 it read as follows: "The lieutenant governor shall receive double the *per diem* allowance of members of the senate, for every day's attendance as president of the senate, and the same mileage as shall be allowed to members of the legislature."

The vice president receives a salary of eight thousand dollars.

SECTION X.

Every bill which shall have passed the legislature shall, before it becomes a law, be presented to the governor. If he approve, he shall sign it; but if not, he shall return it, with his objections, to that house in which it shall have originated, who shall enter the objections at large upon the journal and proceed to reconsider it. If, after such reconsideration, two-thirds of the members present shall agree to pass the bill, it shall be sent, together with the objections to the other house, by which it shall likewise be reconsidered, and if approved by two-thirds of the members present, it shall become a law. But in all such cases, the votes of both houses shall be determined by yeas and nays, and the names of the members voting for or against the bill shall be entered on the journal of each house respectively. If any bill shall not be returned by the governor within three days (Sundays excepted) after it shall have been presented to him, the same shall be a law, unless the legislature shall, by their adjournment, prevent its return; in which case it shall not be a law.*

A bill becomes a law as soon as it is signed by the governor, or if he refuses to sign it as soon as it is passed over his veto.

When the governor vetos a bill, his reasons for vetoing the bill must be given in writing, so that they can be copied upon the journal of the house that originated the bill. They *must* then vote upon it, and they *must* vote by ayes and noes, so that the vote of every member can be recorded. If two-thirds of the members present do not agree to pass it, that is the end of the bill. If two-thirds of the members present do vote for it, it goes to the other house, where the governor's objections are entered upon the journal as before, and a vote taken by ayes and noes, and recorded as before. If two-thirds of the members present do not vote for the bill, the bill is

* This section is taken with a few slight changes from the United States constitution. (I, 7.)

lost. If two-thirds of them do vote for it, it becomes a law.

The president of the United States has ten days in which to consider a bill which has been passed by congress. The governor has only three days in which to consider a bill which has been passed by the legislature. In these three days Sundays are not counted, because no official business can be done on Sunday.

During the last three days of the session of the legislature the governor need not veto a bill that he does not wish to become a law. All he needs to do is not to sign it, and then it cannot become a law, even if two-thirds of each house are ready to vote for it.

There are four ways in which a bill may be lost :

1. It may not get a majority in the assembly ;

2. It may not get a majority in the senate ;

3. It may be vetoed by the governor and not passed over his veto by the legislature ;

4. It may be " pocketed " by the governor during the last three days of the session,

And there are three ways in which a bill may become a law :

1. It may pass both houses and be signed by the governor ;

2. It may pass both houses, be vetoed by the governor, and be passed over his veto by a two-thirds majority of each house;

3. It may pass both houses and the governor may fail to sign it within three days, (when these are not at the close of the session).

ARTICLE VI.

ADMINISTRATIVE.

In addition to the offices created by this article, the office of superintendent of public instruction is created by article X, section 1; and other state offices have been created by acts of the legislature, so that the state administration now consists of the following officers, each at the head of a department, and each elected for a term of two years:*

1. *The Secretary of State.*
2. *The State Treasurer.*
3. *The Attorney General.*
4. *The State Superintendent of Public Instruction.*
5. *The State Commissioner of Immigration.*

In addition to these there are several boards, which virtually form a part of the administration of the state:

1. *The Board of Commissioners for the Sale of School*

---

* The office of state prison commissioner is to be abolished Dec. 31, 1873, a board of three commissioners taking the place of that officer. The office of bank comptroller was abolished Dec. 31, 1869.

and University Lands, consisting of the secretary of state, treasurer and attorney general, whose duties are prescribed in article X, section 8, of the constitution.

2. *The Board of Regents of the State University*, composed of the state superintendent of public instruction, *ex officio*, and twelve persons appointed by the governor.

3. *The Board of Regents of Normal Schools*, composed of the governor and state superintendent of public instruction, who are *ex officio* members, and nine members appointed by the governor with the consent of the senate.

4. *The Board of Commissioners of Charities and Reform.* They have general supervision of the charitable and penal institutions of the state, each of which has its own board of trustees, and which are as follows:

(*a*) The Hospitals for the Insane, located at Madison and Oshkosh.

(*b*) The Institution for the Blind, at Janesville;

(*c*) The Institution for the Deaf and Dumb, at Delavan;

(*d*) The Soldiers' Orphans' Home, at Madison;

(*e*) The Industrial School for Boys, at Waukesha;

(*f*) The State Prison, at Waupun;

This oard also have power to inspect any jail or poor house in the state.

They consist of five persons appointed by the governor, with a secretary elected by the board.

SECTION I.

There shall be chosen by the qualified electors of the state, at the times and places of choosing the members of the legislature, a secretary of state, treasurer and attorney general, who shall severally hold their offices for the term of two years.

All the state officers, including the governor and lieutenant governor, are elected for two years, and the election comes in the odd years, while the election for members of congress comes in the even years, and the election for president in the leap years. No qualifications are required by this section for the administrative officers. But by a decision of the supreme court in the case of a sheriff,* the principle of which would apply also to state officers, state and county officers must be citizens or foreigners who have declared their intention to become citizens.

SECTION II.

The secretary of state shall keep a fair record of the official acts of the legislature and executive department of the state, and shall, when required, lay the same and all matters relative thereto before either branch of the legislature. He shall be *ex officio* auditor and shall perform such other duties as shall be assigned him by law. He shall receive as a compensation for his services, yearly, such sum as shall be provided by law, and shall keep his office at the seat of government.

The secretary of state is not required to keep a record of the judicial department, because such a record is kept by the clerk of each of the courts.

* "It is an acknowledged principle which lies at the very foundation, and the enforcement of which needs neither the aid of statutory or constitutional enactments or restrictions; that the government is instituted by the citizens for their liberty and protection; and that it is to be administered and its powers and functions exercised by them and through their agency." (Wis Reports, vol. xiv., p. 497.)

Foreigners who have declared their intention to become citizens of the United States are citizens of the state.

"An alien who has not declared his intention to become a citizen of the United States may be *elected* to the office of clerk of the county board of supervisors, and in case his disability is removed before the commencement of the term of office for which he is elected, will be entitled to enter upon and hold such office."

"It seems that a minor or a person who has not resided one year in the state, may be elected to public office in this state, and may enter upon the duties of such office in case the disability, as to age or residence, ceases before the term of office for which he is elected commences." (Wis. Reports, vol. xxx., p. 96.) This principle applies to the eligibility of all officers in this state. The persons holding these offices must be eligible, not at the time of being elected or appointed, but at the time of *entering upon* the offices.

As auditor he must examine the accounts of the treasurer and also examine the claims against the state.

SECTION III.

The powers, duties and compensation of the treasurer and attorney general shall be prescribed by law.

The state treasurer keeps the money and accounts of the state; and the attorney general is the lawyer for the state. They each have an office in the capitol at Madison.

SECTION IV.

Sheriffs, coroners, registers of deeds, and district attorneys shall be chosen by the electors of the respective counties, once in every two years, and as often as vacancies shall happen. Sheriffs shall hold no other office, and be ineligible for two years next succeeding the termination of their offices. They may be required by law to renew their security from time to time; and in default of giving such new security, their offices shall be deemed vacant. But the county shall never be made responsible for the acts of the sheriff. The governor may remove any officer in this section mentioned, giving to such officer a copy of the charges against him, and an opportunity of being heard in his defense.

The officers named in this section hold for a full term of two years, and until their successors are elected and qualified, *no matter when their offices begin.** There is only one exception to this, and that is when any of these officers are *appointed* to fill a vacancy, in which case they hold only until their successors are elected and qualified. If they are *elected* to fill a vacancy, they hold for two years from the date of entering upon their office.

*It was so decided by the supreme court in the case of a sheriff, and by parity of reasoning, the principle would apply to the other officers named in this section; but not to other county officers (Simmons' Digest, p. 128; Wis. Reports, Vol. iii, p. 714.) The supreme court has also decided that in a newly organized county where the term of the first officers begin at some other time than the first of January, the sheriff may hold for the full term of two years; and each of his successors may do the same. (Wis. Reports, vol. xiii, p. 168; Simmons' Digest, p. 131.)

The office of sheriff is one of great responsibility, and the constitution provides very carefully against its abuse.

1st. Sheriffs can hold no state office.

2d. They are ineligible *to the office of sheriff** for the next two years, and, therefore, cannot use their office to electioneer for re-election.

3d. They may be required to renew their security from time to time.

4th. The county cannot be made responsible for their acts.

5th. The governor may remove them at any time, for cause.

The supreme court has decided that this section not only provides for the election of sheriffs, but determines their powers and duties.†

In addition to the county officers named in this section, the following are otherwise provided for:

Clerk of the circuit court, (VII, 12).

County judge, (VII, 14).

County clerk, (by statute).

County Treasurer, (by statute).

County surveyor, (by statute).

Superintendent of schools, (by statute, under X, I).

---

* The supreme court has decided that any person holding the office of sheriff is eligible to another county office, the term of which commences when his term as sheriff expires. (Wis. Reports, xiii, 105; Simmons' Digest, iii, 747).

† "Under our state constitution, which provides for the election of sheriffs by the electors of the county, the legislature cannot transfer to other officers, elected by the board of supervisors, important powers and functions which from time immemorial have belonged to the office of sheriff." (Wis. Reports, vol. xxii, p. 412).

ARTICLE VII.

JUDICIARY.

The following additional matters pertaining to the judiciary, given in other parts of this constitution, are added below:

SECTION I.

[1] The court for the trial of impeachments shall be composed of the senate. [2] The house of representatives shall have the power of impeaching [3] all civil officers of this state, [4] for corrupt conduct in office, or for crimes and misdemeanors; but a majority of all the members elected shall concur in an impeachment. [5] On the trial of an impeachment against the governor, the lieutenant governor shall not act as a member of the court. [6] No judicial officer shall exercise his office after he shall have been impeached, until his acquittal. Before the trial of an impeachment, the members of the court shall take an oath or affirmation truly and impartially to try the impeachment, accord-

ing to evidence; ¹and no person shall be convicted without the concurrence of two-thirds of the members present. ²Judgment in cases of impeachment, shall not extend further than to removal from office, or removal from office and disqualification to hold any office of honor, profit or trust, under the state; but the party impeached shall be liable to indictment, trial and punishment according to law.

¹ An impeachment trial is not a common criminal trial; it is a political trial. The offenses which can be tried are political offenses; the persons who can be tried are political officers, and the only punishments which can be imposed are political punishments. And, therefore, the court which tries them is the highest political body in the state.* But the trial is carried on according to the usual forms and methods of higher courts of law, for the senate is then sitting as a court and not as a legislative body.

² The name, house of representatives, evidently stands for the assembly, by an unusual piece of carelessness in the framers of the constitution. The lower house of the legislature has the power of impeachment, because it represents the people more directly than any other part of the state government, being elected every year. An impeachment by the assembly answers to a presentment by a grand jury in criminal cases. It puts the person impeached upon his trial; but it does not necessarily follow because an officer is impeached that he is therefore convicted.

It is a common mistake to talk of the impeachment of an officer as if that were the same as conviction.

³ The persons who can be impeached are the civil offi-

---

* "An impeachment is a proceeding purely of a political nature. It is not so much a design to punish an offender as to secure the state against gross official misdemeanors. It touches neither his person or his property; but simply divests him of his political capacity." Story, § 793.

cers of the state. Military officers cannot be impeached; but they can be tried by court martial and cashiered for corrupt conduct in office. Nor can members of the legislature be impeached. They are not officers of the state but representatives of the people.*

Senators and assemblymen can be expelled for the same offenses for which civil officers can be impeached.

Judges may be impeached, but they may also be removed by address (VII, 13).

'An officer may be impeached for corrupt conduct in office or for crimes and misdemeanors which show that he is not a fit person to be entrusted with office. Treason, bribery, gross neglect of duty, direct disobedience of the laws, and the like, would be considered corrupt conduct in office.

The crimes and misdemeanors for which an officer may be impeached are not exactly defined by the constitution, and it was not intended they should be. The assembly must decide upon each case that comes up whether it is worthy of impeachment or not; and the senate whether the person impeached deserves to be removed from office or not.

⁵ The lieutenant governor presides over the senate at all impeachment trials, except when the governor is impeached. In that case, he has a direct interest in the result of the trial, for he would become governor if the governor should be removed; and, moreover, he is then

---

* The United States senate decided on an impeachment trial in 1799, that a senator is not a civil officer of the United States, and cannot be impeached. There is no instance in England or America of a legislator being impeached. See Story on the constitution, § 793-5. The constitution of Wisconsin favors this view by making all acts of the legislature begin, "The people of the state of Wisconsin represented in senate and assembly do enact as follows," which implies that senators and assemblymen are not officers of the state but representatives of the people.

acting governor and cannot perform both functions at once. When the governor is impeached, or if for any other cause the lieutenant governor does not preside, the senate elects a president from its own members.

⁶ Under the United States constitution impeached officers still continue to act in their offices until removed by the sentence of the senate, and the same rule holds in Wisconsin. An exception, however, is made with regard to judicial officers, and also with regard to the governor, (V, 7).

⁷ The state constitution follows the United States constitution in requiring a two-thirds majority to convict. Otherwise a partizan majority might impeach and remove a governor or other officers for party purposes.

⁸ The persons who can be tried are officers of the state. They can be tried only for political offenses, and their punishment is political. It may only be removal from office, and it may also be disqualification for office ever after. This disqualification can be removed at any time by act of the legislature. If the offense is also a criminal offense as well as a political offense, the officer may be tried by the ordinary courts and punished at any time.

The state has, therefore, three methods of procedure against an unworthy officer:

1st. He can be impeached and removed from office, and also disqualified from holding any office under the state.

2d. If guilty of a criminal offense, he can be indicted, tried and punished like any other criminal.

3d. If he has wrongfully taken money or property from the state, it can be recovered by a civil process.

SECTION II.

The judicial power of this state, [1] both as to matters of law and equity, shall be vested in a supreme court, circuit courts, courts of probate and in justices of the peace. [2] The legislature may also vest such jurisdiction as shall be deemed necessary in municipal courts, and shall have power to establish inferior courts, in the several counties, with limited civil and criminal jurisdiction. *Provided*, that the jurisdiction which may be vested in municipal courts shall not exceed, in their respective municipalities, that of circuit courts in their respective circuits, as prescribed in this constitution; and that the legislature shall provide as well for the election of judges of the municipal courts as of the judges of inferior courts, by the qualified electors of the respective jurisdictions. The term of office of the judges of the said municipal and inferior courts shall not be longer than that of the judges of the circuit courts.

[1] In England and in some of the states of our Union there are two sets of courts to try two classes of cases, called law cases and equity cases. The same courts try both classes of cases here. (See comments on section 19.)

[2] The legislature has established police courts in several cities by their charters, and has also given common law jurisdiction to probate courts in several counties, by the authority of this section. The judicial power of the state is vested in the courts named in this section, and in these alone.*

SECTION III.

[1] The supreme court, except in cases otherwise provided in this constitution, shall have appellate jurisdiction only, which shall be co-extensive with the state; but in no case removed to the supreme court, shall a trial by jury be allowed. [2] The supreme court shall have a general superintending control over all inferior courts; it shall have power to issue writs of [3] habeas corpus, [4] mandamus, [5] injunction, [6] quo warranto, [7] certiorari and other original and remedial writs, and to hear and determine the same.

* "Under our state constitution the legislature cannot vest in any officer or body other than the courts therein provided for, any *judicial* powers to be finally and exclusively exercised by such officer or body." (Wis. Reports. vol. xxvii, p. 119).

¹ The only cases in which the supreme court has original jurisdiction are those of suits against the state, and
the original writs named below.

In all other cases suits must first be brought before
some inferior courts; and an appeal may be taken from
its decision to the next higher court, and so on until it
reaches the supreme court where a decision is final. No
jury is allowed in the supreme court; but all questions
of fact must be decided by jury; therefore, when a suit
is brought against the state in the supreme court, the
evidence is heard before a jury empanelled in some circuit court, and then the supreme court decides upon the
law of the case thus made up. But, in case of appeal
from a circuit court, the same evidence that was taken
before the circuit court is used over again.

The facts upon which the case is to be decided remain
the same as they were proved before the circuit court, but
the law of the case is argued over again by the lawyers
on each side, and is decided on by the supreme court.

The decisions of the supreme court in regard to the
law of any case, are always followed by all lower courts
in all like cases, and are usually followed afterward by
the supreme court, though not always. The decisions
of the supreme court interpret the law, and, therefore,
in a certain sense, the supreme court may be said to
sometimes make laws. Where a law may be understood
to mean several different things, every court must decide for itself what it real'y does mean; and as the
supreme court is the final and highest authority, its decision decides finally the meaning of the law in dispute,
unless that decision is afterward reversed by the supreme
court itself.

A similar power is that of deciding laws to be uncon-stitutional. All the statute laws of the state are, of course, subject to the constitution of the state, and to the constitution and statutes and treaties of the United States. Upon any case coming before any court in the state the plea may be made by the lawyers on either side, that a certain law or part of a law bearing on that case is unconstitutional, or that it is an encroachment on the supreme authority of the United States, as expressed in its constitution, statutes or treaties with foreign pow-ers. If the plea is sustained by the court, and the de-cision is not reversed by a higher court, that law or part of law is ever after regarded in all courts as void and good for nothing. A decision in the supreme court is the highest authority upon the constitutionality of a law.

[2] The supreme court exercises this general control over inferior courts, by reason of the right of appeal and of writs of error (I, 21), and by reason of the writs named in this section.* These writs are all named from the Latin words with which they begin, for these writs were formerly in England issued in Latin. Those mentioned

---

* "The intent of Article VII, section 3, of our constitution, was not so much to give the supreme court power to issue a writ of a prescribed form, as to enable it to hear and determine controversies of a certain character; and this jurisdiction cannot be taken away by any legislative change in the form of the remedy; but the court may adopt any new process which is cal-culated to attain the same end." (Simmons' Digest, p. 089; Wis. Reports, vol. xvi, p. 115).

" In these writs the supreme court has original jurisdiction, that is, a writ of *habeas corpus* or *mandamus*, or *injunction*, or *quo warranto*, can be con-stitutionally issued from the supreme court, as well as from a circuit court." (Wis. Reports, vol. i, p. 317, vol. lii, p. 1 and 157; Simmons' Digest, p. 120).

In ordinary cases, however, the supreme court refuses to grant these writs, and refers the petitioners to the circuit court. It is only in exceptional cases that the supreme court will grant the writs named above.

" The supreme court has authority to issue a common law writ of certiorari to bring before itself a judgment rendered by a justice of the peace, but it will not do so in ordinary cases, where there is an opportunity to apply for such writ to the circuit court of the proper county, in time to avoid the threatened injury to the party applying." (Simmons' Digest, p. 770; Chand-ler's Reports, vol. i, p. 285).

here are the most important writs used by the courts to secure justice, and are used as follows:

 ¹ The writ of *habeas corpus* (you may have the body) commands the person to whom it is issued to produce the body of some person who it is charged he holds in unjust confinement, before the court, and show cause why he should not be liberated. If an officer holds a prisoner without a warrant for his arrest, or if he is held in prison longer than he should be held, or, if excessive bail is required, the prisoner can be liberated by a writ of *habeas corpus.* So also where a private person, not parent or guardian, holds a child, he can be released by a writ of habeas corpus.*

 ⁴ The writ of *mandamus* (we command) commands officers and others to do certain things which it is their duty to do. For instance, if the secretary of state should refuse to give a certificate of election to a member of the legislature duly elected, and he could not take his seat because of it, the circuit or supreme court would issue a writ of *mandamus* and compel the certificate to be given.†

 ⁵A writ of *injunction* forbids certain things to be done, which, if done, would cause injury which could not be remedied by the law, or commands certain things to be done, the neglect of which would cause an injury which could not be remedied.‡

---

* For decisions about the writ of *habeas corpus* see note to article 1st, section 8.

†"A writ of mandamus is the highest judicial writ known to our constitution and laws, and is only issued in cases where there is a specific legal right to be enforced, or where there is a positive duty to be performed, which can be performed, and where there is no other specific legal remedy." (Simmons' Digest, p. 501; Chandlers' Reports, vol. ii, p. 247.)
 "Where the law vests a discretion in any officer or body with reference to any subject, such discretion will not be controlled by mandamus." (Simmons' Digest, p. 501; Wis. Reports, vol. ix, p. 254.)

‡"The granting or refusal of injunctions rests in the sound discretion of the

⁶A writ of *quo warranto* (by what warrant) is one which calls upon a person or corporation to show by what authority he or it exercises certain powers.* For instance, on the first of January, 1856, the governor elect sued out a writ of *quo warranto* in the supreme court, against his predecessor, who refused to give up the office, and was put into the office by the power of the supreme court.

⁷A writ of *certiorari* (to be certified of) is very much the same thing as a writ of error. When a higher court is certified or assured that justice is not being done in some case in a lower court, such a writ will be issued, and the case removed to the higher court. This writ compels the lower court to send up the record of a case that has been tried or is being tried in the lower court; and then the higher court tries the case upon the facts shown in the record.

SECTION IV.

[For the term of five years, and thereafter until the legislature shall otherwise provide, the judges of the several circuit courts shall be judges of the supreme court, four of whom shall constitute a quorum, and the concurrence of a majority of the judges present shall be necessary to a decision.] The legislature shall have power, if they should think it expedient and necessary, to provide by law for the organization of a separate supreme court with the jurisdiction and powers prescribed in this

court. They are never granted when they would be against conscience or productive of hardship, oppression, injustice, or public or private mischief." (Simmons' Digest. p. 4 7: Wis. Reports, vol. ix, p. 166, vol. xiv, p. 618 and p. 443, and vol. xvi, p. 661.)

"Although the writ of injunction is abolished by chapter 129, revised statutes, yet the remedy is retained and the power of courts to grant that peculiar relief is enlarged, rather than abridged." (Simmons' Digest, p. 405; Wis. Reports, vol. xiii, p. 348.)

* "Both the common law writ of *quo warranto*, and the proceeding by information which was substituted therefor, were abolished by the code (chapter 160 of the Revised Statutes), and the remedies before to be obtained in those forms, are now to be sought and obtained by a civil action, to be commenced and prosecuted in all respects like other civil actions." (Simmons' Digest, p. 689; Wis. Reports, vol. xiv, p. 115).

The question which of two contestants is entitled to hold a certain office, has been frequently tried before the supreme court.

constitution, to consist of one chief justice and two associate justices, to be elected by the qualified electors of the state, at such time
and in such manner as the legislature may provide.   The separate supreme court, when so organized, shall not be changed or
discontinued by the legislature; the judges thereof shall be so
classified that but one of them shall go out of office at the same
time, and their term of office shall be the same as provided for the
judges of the circuit court. [And whenever the legislature may
consider it necessary to establish a separate supreme court, they
shall have the power to reduce the number of circuit judges to
four, and subdivide the judicial circuits, but no such subdivis-
ion or reduction shall take effect until after the expiration of
the term of some one of the said judges, or until a vacancy occur by some other means.]*

The legislature has so reorganized the supreme court.
It now consists of a chief justice and two associate justices, who are each elected for a term of six years, one
of them every two years.   The time of election for
judges of the supreme and circuit courts is at the town
elections in the spring, the first Tuesday in April.

SECTIONS V† AND VI.

The legislature may alter the limits, or increase the number of
circuits, making them as compact and convenient as practicable,
and bounding them by county lines, but no such alteration or
increase shall have the effect to remove a judge from office.   In
case of an increase of circuits, the judge . or judges shall be
elected as provided in this constitution, and receive a salary not
less than that herein provided for judges of the circuit court.

The legislature has frequently altered and increased
the circuits.   The counties composing the circuits and

*The parts of this section printed in brackets are no longer in force.
†Section 5 is no longer in force. It is therefore omitted in the text. It
reads as follows:
"The state shall be divided into five judicial circuits, to be composed as
follows: The first circuit shall comprise the counties of Racine, Walworth,
Rock and Green. The second circuit, the counties of Milwaukee, Waukesha,
Jefferson and Dane. The third circuit, the counties of Washington, Dodge,
Columbia, Marquette, Sauk and Portage. The fourth circuit, the counties of
Brown, Manitowoc, Sheboygan, Fond du Lac, Winnebago and Calumet. And
the fifth circuit shall comprise the counties of Iowa, La Fayette, Grant, Crawford and St. Croix; and the county of Richland shall be attached to Iowa,
the county of Chippewa to the county of Crawford, and the county of La
Pointe to the county of St. Croix, for judicial purposes, until otherwise provided by the legislature."

the judges of each can be learned from any legislative manual. There are now twelve judicial circuits.

SECTION VII.

For each circuit there shall be a judge chosen by the qualified electors therein, who shall hold his office as is provided in this constitution, and until his successor shall be chosen and qualified; and after he shall have been elected. he shall reside in the circuit for which he was elected.*

Every circuit judge must live in his own circuit, because there are a great many writs and processes that he may have to issue when he is not holding court, and it would be very inconvenient to go out of the circuit after · him, to have a writ issued.

Judges are now always elected for six years, unless it is to fill a vacancy, when they are elected for the rest of the term of the judge whose place is to be filled. (Sec. 9.)

SECTION VIII.

The circuit courts shall have original jurisdiction in all matters, civil and criminal, within this state, not excepted in this constitution, and not hereafter prohibited by law, and appellate jurisdiction from all inferior courts and tribunals, and a supervisory control over the same. They shall also have the power to issue writs of habeas corpus, mandamus, injunction, quo warranto, certiorari,† and all other writs necessary to carry into effect their orders, judgments and decrees, and give them a general control over inferior courts and jurisdictions.

All important cases begin in some circuit court; small cases begin before a justice of the peace, or a police magistrate, or a county judge and may be appealed to

---

*The rest of this section was made obsolete when a separate supreme court was organized. It reads as follows:

"One of said judges shall be designated as chief justice, in such manner as the legislature shall provide. And the legislature shall, at its first session, provide by law, as well for the election of as for classifying the judges of the circuit court, to be elected under this constitution, in such a manner that one of said judges shall go out of office in two years, one in three years, one in four years. one in five years and one in six years, and thereafter the judge elected to fill the office shall hold the same for six years."

† See the definitions of these writs under section 3.

the circuit court* or carried up on a writ of error or of certiorari, if either party is aggrieved at a decision made in the lower court. Each circuit court has jurisdiction in its own district and in that only, except in two cases:

1st. Crimes and misdemeanors committed on lake Michigan, lake Superior, lake Winnebago and the Mississippi and St. Croix rivers, may be tried in the courts of any county that borders on them. (See comments on IX, 1.)

2d. Cases may be changed from one county to another or one circuit to another, when it is likely that the trial would not be fair in the county or circuit where they were begun. This is called a change of venue. (See I, 7.)

SECTION IX.

[1] When a vacancy shall happen in the office of judge of the supreme or circuit courts, such vacancy shall be filled by an appointment of the governor, which shall continue until a successor is elected and qualified; and when elected, such successor shall hold his office the residue of the unexpired term. [2] There shall be no election for a judge or judges at any general election for state or county officers, nor within thirty days either before or after such election.

[1] A vacancy may occur in a judgeship by the death or resignation of the judge, by his accepting any other office whatever, by his removing his residence, if a circuit judge, outside his circuit; and if a supreme judge, outside the state; or, by his removal from office by impeachment or address. If a judge is impeached by the assembly, he is suspended from his office until his trial is through. If not convicted he resumes his office.

[2] The state and county elections are held in the fall.

* "A statute which authorizes appeals to be taken directly from a county court to the supreme court in civil cases, is not in violation of sec. 8, art. vii, of the state constitution." (Wis. Reports, vol. xxx, p. 434.)

The election of judges of the supreme court and circuit court are held in the spring at the town elections. The reason of this is, so that the political and party feeling which is rife at the state and county elections, should not influence the nomination or election of the judges. They ought to be elected for their fitness for the place, and not for their party services.*

SECTION X.

[1]Each of the judges of the supreme and circuit courts shall receive a salary, payable quarterly, of not less than one thousand five hundred dollars annually; [2]they shall receive no fees of office, or other compensation than their salaries; [3]they shall hold no office of public trust, except a judicial office, during the term for which they are respectively elected, and all votes for either of them, for any office except a judicial office, given by the legislature or the people, shall be void. [4]No person shall be eligible to the office of judge, who shall not, at the time of his election, be a citizen of the United States, and have attained the age of twenty-five years, and be a qualified elector within the jurisdiction for which he may be chosen.

[1] The salary of circuit judges is now $3,000 ; that of judges of the supreme court, $5,000.

[2] If judges received fees or other compensation it might often influence their decisions upon cases before them, or at least give rise to the suspicion that the decisions were so influenced.

[3] A judge should have no interests of any sort except to render strict and impartial justice ; his whole time must be given to this. Therefore, he is not allowed to hold any other office or even to electioneer for another better office while he is a judge. If it were not for this provision a judge might run for congress or for the

* "The provision that prohibits a judicial election at any general election, applies only to supreme and circuit judges, and not to probate and county judges, or justices of the peace." (See Simmons' Digest, p. 248, and Chandler's Reports, vol. i, p. 130). Nevertheless, the election for these inferior judicial officers are all held at the spring election.

senate, while he was judge, expecting to resign his judgeship if elected. But this is effectually stopped by making all votes for him void.

‘No other state officer need be more than twenty-one years old, but a judge must be twenty-five years old. He must have lived at least one year in the state to be a qualified elector. He must live in the state if a judge of the supreme court, and in his circuit if a circuit judge, to be a qualified elector in the jurisdiction for which he is chosen. If of foreign birth, he must have lived in the United States at least five years to be a citizen of the United States.

SECTION XI.

¹ The supreme court shall hold at least one term annually, at the seat of government of the state, at such time as shall be provided by law, and the legislature may provide for holding other terms, and at other places, when they may deem it necessary. ² A circuit court shall be held at least twice in each year, in each county of this state, organized for judicial purposes. ³ The judges of the circuit court may hold courts for each other, and shall do so when required by law.

¹ The sessions of the supreme court are held twice a year at Madison in the capitol.

² The sessions of the circuit court are always held at the county seat of each county. Four sessions are held in Milwaukee county and three in several other counties. Two sessions are held in all the others, except where the county is new and thinly populated. In that case, the legislature attaches it to some neighboring county for judicial purposes, and all cases are tried at the county seat of the latter county. Instances of this are to be seen in section 5 of this article. Thus Richland county was attached to Iowa county for judicial purposes; that

is, all suits before the circuit court, by people in Richland county, were to be tried at the term of court held in Iowa county.

[3] If for any reason a judge cannot hold court at a certain time and place, he may get some other judge to hold court for him at that time and place. This can be done when a judge is sick or has some other private reason which stops his doing business.

SECTION XII.

There shall be a clerk of the circuit court chosen in each county organized for judicial purposes, by the qualified electors thereof, who shall hold his office for two years, subject to removal, as shall be provided by law. In case of a vacancy, the judge of the circuit court shall have the power to appoint a clerk, until the vacancy shall be filled by an election. The clerk thus elected or appointed shall give such security as the legislature may require; and when elected, shall hold his office for a full term. The supreme court shall appoint its own clerk, and the clerk of the circuit court may be appointed clerk of the supreme court.

Where a county is not organized for judicial purposes, it is attached to some neighboring county for judicial purposes, and the clerk of the court in that county, is clerk of the court for both. The clerk of the court may be removed by the circuit judge at any time; but he must have a copy of the charges against him, and an opportunity to be heard in his own defense.

When a clerk of the circuit court dies or resigns, or is removed, the judge appoints a clerk in his place, and the person so appointed is clerk the rest of the year. Should the vacancy happen in the second year of the clerk's office, another clerk is elected, of course, at the next fall election, whose office begins the first of the next January. But should the vacancy happen in the first year of his office, a clerk will be elected at the election held that fall, and will hold office for two years. The year for electing the clerk of the circuit court, in that county, will thus be changed from an even year to an odd year, or from an odd year to an even year, as the case may be.

SECTION XIII.

Any judge of the supreme or circuit court may be removed from office by address of both houses of the legislature, if two-thirds of al' the members elect to each house concur therein, but no removal shall be made by virtue of this section, unless the judge complained of shall have been served with a copy of the charges against him as the ground of address, and shall have had an opportunity of being heard in his defense. On the question of removal, the ayes and noes shall be entered on the journals.

This is a shorter method of removing a bad judge than by impeachment; but it requires a larger majority of the legislature to do it.

A removal by impeachment requires a majority of all the members elected to the assembly and two-thirds of all present in the senate. While a removal by address requires two-thirds of all the members elected to each house. But in case of a flagrant offense, this saves the long formalities of a trial. Substantial justice is provided for, in giving the accused judge a copy of the charges against him and allowing him to be heard in his defense, and in requiring the members to vote by ayes and noes. The address is made to the governor who thereupon removes the judge and appoints some one to fill the vacancy thus made.

SECTION XIV.

There shall be chosen in each county, by the qualified electors thereof, a judge of probate, who shall hold his office for two years, and until his successor shall be elected and qualified, and

H

whose jurisdiction, powers and duties shall be prescribed by law. *Provided, however*, that the legislature shall have power to abolish the office of judge of probate in any county, and to confer probate powers upon such inferior courts as may be established in said county.

The probate judges are called also county judges. Their jurisdiction extends to all cases of wills and inheritance of property, and guardianship of moneys, and administration of the estate of deceased persons. The legislature has given the county courts jurisdiction in civil cases, in several counties, under section 2.

SECTION XV.

The electors of the several towns, at their annual town meetings, and the electors of cities and villages, at their charter elections, shall, in such manner as the legislature may direct, elect justices of the peace, whose term of office shall be for two years, and until their successors in office shall be elected and qualified. In case of an election to fill a vacancy occurring before the expiration of a full term, the justice elected shall hold for the residue of the unexpired term. Their number and classifications shall be regulated by law. And the tenure of two years shall in no wise interfere with the classification in the first instance. The justices thus elected shalll have such civil and criminal jurisdiction as shall be prescribed by law.

There are four justices of the peace elected in every town, two each year, at the spring election. If there is a vacancy for any cause it is filled at the next spring election.

Justices have jurisdiction anywhere in their county in civil suits of all cases where the value in controversy is less than two hundred dollars, and in criminal cases in minor offenses. The sentence of a justice of the peace can be appealed from to the next higher court in all cases.

SECTION XVI.

The legislature shall pass laws for the regulation of tribunals of conciliation, defining their powers and duties. Such tribunals may be established in and for any township, and shall have power to render judgment, to be obligatory on the parties, when they shall voluntarily submit their matter in difference to arbitration, and agree to abide the judgment, or assent thereto in writing.

The legislature has established no regular tribunals of conciliation. But the law allows parties to a civil suit, who choose to do so, to submit their difference to arbitrators, chosen by both of them. These arbitrators are for that particular case a " tribunal of conciliation."

This section of the constitution evidently means more than this, and the legislature has neglected its duty in not establishing these " tribunals of conciliation " in every township. If such tribunals were established, half the law-suits, with the expenses and hatred involved in them, would be saved.

SECTION XVII.

The style of all writs and process shall be, "The state of Wisconsin." All criminal prosecutions shall be carried on in the name and by the authority of the same; and all indictments shall conclude against the peace and dignity of the state.

Thus, every constable and justice of the peace represents the state of Wisconsin within his own jurisdiction. And the sovereign authority of the state is extended to every official action of the officers of the law throughout the state.

Every writ and process must begin with the words "The state of Wisconsin," and every indictment, after stating the offense with which the accused is charged, must conclude with the words "against the peace and dignity of the state of Wisconsin."*

* "An indictment in a court of this state which does not conclude " against the peace and dignity of the state of Wisconsin," is bad, and the words "against the peace of the state of Wisconsin," are not sufficient." (Wis, Reports, vol. xxvii, p. 402.)

SECTION XVIII.

The legislature shall impose a tax on all civil suits commenced or prosecuted in the municipal, inferior, or circuit courts, which shall constitute a fund to be applied toward the payment of the salary of the judges.

The justices of the peace and police magistrates are paid by the fees they receive. The circuit judges receive a salary (sec. 10). A tax of $1.00 is levied on every civil suit in a circuit court, which goes toward the salary of the judge. He accounts to the state treasurer for all fees received, and gets the rest of his salary in a draft on the state treasurer.

SECTION XIX.

The testimony in causes in equity shall be taken in like manner as in cases at law; and the office of master in chancery is hereby prohibited.

The distinction between common law and equity is in form abolished by the code of the state, but still there are differences in substance well understood by lawyers, but too many and too intricate to admit of a definition, or description in the limits of this work. The office of master in chancery in those states in which there are separate courts of equity, answers to the office of court commissioner in courts of law. Under the constitution, the court commissioners perform most of the duties of masters in chancery. The practice of law is greatly simplified by this, and many of the abuses of the English courts of chancery are abolished.

SECTION XX.

Any suitor in any court in this state shall have the right to prosecute or defend his suit either in his own proper person or by an attorney or agent of his choice.

This is a similar provision for civil suits to that made for criminal cases in article I, section 7. Only in criminal cases a lawyer will be furnished by the court, if the defendant is too poor to pay one; but in civil cases each party must pay his lawyer or go without. But every man has a right to be his own lawyer if he chooses.

SECTION XXI.

The legislature shall provide by law for the speedy publication of all statute laws, and of such judicial decisions made within the state, as may be deemed expedient. And no general law shall be in force until published.

It would not be right to punish people for disobeying laws they have no means of knowing. The general laws passed at each session are published in nearly every newspaper in the state, and are also published as a book for the libraries of lawyers. It is presumed that people read the newspapers, and therefore, publication in the newspapers of the state is supposed to be notice enough to all the people of the state. A general law may, however, be made to come into force at some fixed time *later* than its publication.*

The private and local laws are published in a bound volume for the use of courts and lawyers. The decisions of the supreme court are regularly published in the official paper of the state, and in a series of volumes. These are published because they have the force of law; being interpretations of the law which are accepted by all the courts of the state. (See comments on sec. 3).

* "An act of the legislature complete in itself, but which is to take effect only on the happening of a certain contingency,is not invalid for that reason." (Wis. Reports, vol. xxiv, p. 149.)
"An act of the legislature affecting the people of the whole state is not invalid, because by its terms it was to take effect only after it should be approved by a majority of the popular vote at a certain election." (Wis. Reports, vol. xxvi, p. 291.)

SECTION XXII.

The legislature, at its first session after the adoption of this constitution, shall provide for the appointment of three commissioners, whose duty it shall be to inquire into, revise and simplify the rules of practice, pleadings, forms, and proceedings, and arrange a system adapted to the courts of record of this state, and report the same to the legislature, subject to their modification and adoption; and such commission shall terminate upon the rendering of the report, unless otherwise provided by law.

Such a commission was appointed, who reported a code of practice for the courts of this state, which embodies all the improvements upon the common law that are granted by this constitution, and many more. This code was adopted, and all the practice of courts in this state is in accordance with it. The design of the code is to do away with technicalities in the practice of the courts as far as possible, except such as are needed to secure the ends of justice.

SECTION XXIII.

The legislature may provide for the appointment of one or more persons in each organized county, and may vest in such persons such judicial powers as shall be prescribed by law. *Provided*, that said power shall not exceed that of a judge of the circuit court at chambers.

These officers are called court commissioners. By organized county is meant, a county organized for judicial purposes. The judge of each circuit cannot be in every county in his circuit at once, and these court commissioners act as his deputies. They cannot try cases, for that is reserved for the judge at the regular term of court. But they have all the powers of a court of chambers, that is, of a judge when he is not holding a regular court.

ARTICLE VIII.

FINANCE.

SECTION I.

The rule of taxation shall be uniform, and taxes shall be levied upon such property as the legislature shall prescribe.

To make taxation uniform three things are needed: *First*, that the same things should be taxed and the same things exempt from taxation all over the state; which is the case. *Second*, that the value of property should be assessed alike; and this is done as nearly as possible, though it is never done perfectly. *Third*, that the percentage of taxation should be the same; which is the case.

All state taxes are divided equally upon the assessed valuation of the whole state. All county taxes upon the assessed valuation of each county, and all town, village and city taxes upon the assessed valuation of the town, village or city.

SECTION II.

No money shall be paid out of the treasury except in pursuance of an appropriation by law.

That is, the state treasurer has no right to pay out any money, except as he is authorized to do so by the legislature.   There are certain regular expenses of the state government for which an appropriation has been made once for all.   These expenses are paid yearly without any special appropriation; other appropriations are made when needed.

SECTION III.

The credit of the state shall never be given or loaned in aid of any individual, association or corporation.*

The constitution wisely prohibits the state from lending its credit.   Some of the states of our union which have lent their credit to railroads and other corporations have had to pay the debts of these concerns, caused by their mismanagement and final bankruptcy.

SECTION IV.

The state shall never contract any public debt, except in the cases and manner herein provided.

The provisions of the constitution which follow, relating to the state debt, are very wise.   They have kept our state more free from debt than any other state of our union.

SECTION V.

The legislature shall provide for an annual tax sufficient to defray the estimated expenses of the state for each year; and whenever the expenses of any year shall exceed the income, the legislature shall provide for levying a tax for the ensuing year, sufficient, with other sources of income, to pay the deficiency, as well as the estimated expenses of such ensuing year.

*"The supreme court has decided that although the state is forbidden from lending its credit, it can authorize cities, counties, towns and villages to lend their credit." (Wis. Reports, vol. vii, p. 688, vol. x, p. 136 and 195. Simmons' Digest, p. 134.)

The ordinary expenses of each year must be paid by the year's taxes. They cannot be made a debt upon the state. But if for any cause, there should be a deficit in any year, it must be paid by the taxes of the next year. The deficit must not go on increasing from year to year.

SECTION VI.

For the purpose of defraying extraordinary expenses, the state may contract public debts; but such debts shall never in the aggregate exceed one hundred thousand dollars. Every such debt shall be authorized by law, for some purpose or purposes to be distinctly specified therein; and the vote of a majority of all the members elected to each house, to be taken by yeas and nays, shall be necessary to the passage of such law; and every such law shall provide for levying an annual tax sufficient to pay the annual interest of such debt, and the principal within five years from the passage of such law, and shall specially appropriate the proceeds of such taxes to the payment of such principal and interest; and such appropriation shall not be repealed, nor the taxes be postponed or diminished, until the principal and interest of such debt shall have been wholly paid.

The power of the legislature to run the state in debt is very carefully guarded:

First. No other branch of the government can run the state in debt.

Second. The debt can only be for extraordinary expenses, not for the regular annual expenses of carrying on the government.

Third. These debts altogether shall never exceed $100,000 at any one time.

Fourth. If the legislature authorizes such a debt, it must be by law, and the purpose for which the money is to be borrowed must be distinctly stated in the law.

Fifth. When the law is voted in either house, three-fifths of the members must be present to make a quorum (sec. 8), and a majority of all the members elected must vote for it; that is, as the number now stands, in the assembly, at least, fifty-one members must vote for the bill; and in the senate at least seventeen.

Sixth. The vote must be taken by yeas and nays, and, of course, the vote of each member recorded on the journal so that any one may know how he voted.

Seventh. Every law that makes a debt must provide for paying it, interest and principal in five years.

Eighth. The payment of the debt cannot be put off, but the taxes must be raised every year that shall pay it in five years at the farthest.

These provisions of the constitution have kept the state from having a heavy debt. There are few states of our union whose credit is so good, and whose debt is so small as Wisconsin.

SECTION VII.

[1]The legislature may also borrow money to repel invasion, suppress insurrection, or defend the state in time of war; [2]but the money thus raised shall be applied exclusively to the object for which the loan was authorized, or to the repayment of the debt thereby created.

[1] War is a very costly luxury, and the expenses of a war cannot be paid in the same year, as the ordinary expenses of the state government can. The expenses of a war must be paid mostly from borrowed money. Therefore, the constitution allows the legislature to contract a debt for war expenses. But the war must be a defensive war. The state cannot carry on an offensive war; that is a power which the United States reserves to itself. But the state may be obliged to defend itself against insurrection by rebels at home or invasion by a foreign foe, or may have to prevent invasion by de-

fending itself beyond its own frontier. In that case the state can carry on war.

¹ The legislature may borrow money to pay the expenses of a defensive war, and thus create a war debt. It may also borrow money, if need be, to pay the debt ' when it is due, and thus keep up a debt which is really the same debt with the time of payment extended.

SECTION VIII.

On the passage in either house of the legislature, of any law which imposes, continues, or renews a tax, or creates a debt or charge, or makes, continues, or renews an appropriation of public or trust money, or releases, discharges, or commutes a claim or demand of the state, the question shall be taken by yeas and nays, which shall be duly entered on the journal; and three-fifths of all the members elected to such house, shall in all such cases be required to constitute a quorum therein.

Every vote upon a question in which money is concerned must be a matter of public record, so that any one can tell at any time how any member of the legislature voted upon any such question. Members feel their responsibility more when their votes are taken by yeas and nays and entered upon the journal.

SECTION IX.

No scrip, certificate, or other evidence of state debt whatsoever, shall be issued, except for such debts as are authorized by the sixth and seventh sections of this article.

The state officers have no right to issue certificates of debt, or anything that shall bind the state in any way, except they are authorized to do so by a vote of the legislature, and the legislature itself has no right to authorize any debt except such as are authorized by sections 6 and 7.

SECTION X.

[1] The state shall never contract any debt for works of internal improvement, or be a party in carrying on such works; [2] but whenever grants of land or other property shall have been made to the state, especially dedicated by the grant to particular works of internal improvement, the state may carry on such particular works, and shall devote thereto the avails of such grants, and may pledge or appropriate the revenues derived from such works in aid of their completion.

[1] Works of internal improvement are such as railroads, canals, roads, bridges, the drainage of swamps, and the like. If the state should undertake such works as these it would be sure to run into debt; and it would be very possible that the money would not be wisely expended. Experience has shown that private persons and companies can do such work better than governments can.

[2] An exception is made, where grants have been made by the United States or otherwise, to the state to carry on improvements. In that case the state is only a trustee to carry out the wishes of the government or persons who gave the property. The state has done this with the swamp lands given it by the United States. Half the proceeds of these are used to drain the other swamp lands.

ARTICLE IX.

EMINENT DOMAIN AND PROPERTY OF THE STATE.

(For analysis see article II.)

SECTION I.

[1]The state shall have concurrent jurisdiction on all lakes and rivers bordering on this state, so far as such rivers or lakes shall form a common boundary to the state, and any other state or territory now or hereafter to be formed and bounded by the same. [2]And the river Mississippi and the navigable waters leading into the Mississippi and St. Lawrence, and the carrying places between the same, shall be common highways, and forever free, as well to the inhabitants of the state as to the citizens of the United States, without any tax, impost or duty therefor.

[1] The state has sole jurisdiction within its own boundaries on land ; no other state has any jurisdiction there. But where a river or lake makes a part of the boundary of the state it is not easy to tell where the exact boundary is. It saves some trouble and settles some vexatious questions to give all the states that border on lake Michigan, for instance, each the same jurisdiction anywhere on the lake. There is nothing to tax on the lake except the ships and boats, and these are taxed where they are owned, so that the only things that are affected by the question of jurisdiction, on the lakes and rivers, are the crimes and misdemeanors committed on these rivers and lakes. These may be tried in the courts of any state that border on the lake. For instance, suppose a murder is committed on a steamboat that is going from Milwaukee to Grand Haven, in Michigan when the boat is only a few miles out from Milwaukee. It would be very inconvenient if, because the murder was committed in the waters belonging to Wisconsin, the Wisconsin courts alone had jurisdiction over that

murder. If that were so the boat would either have to turn back to Milwaukee again, and that would cause the passengers a great deal of inconvenience, or else the murderer would get off without any punishment, because the Michigan courts would have no jurisdiction. Or, suppose a crime was committed near the middle of the lake, it would be a delicate question which state had jurisdiction of the offense, because it would be hard to tell just where the boundary line was. But as it now is all the states that border on lake Michigan have concurrent jurisdiction. That is, an offense committed on lake Michigan may be tried before the courts of Wisconsin, of Illinois, of Indiana or of Michigan, whichever is most convenient. So, also, with lake Superior. So, also, with offenses on the Mississippi river, when that river forms the boundary between this state and Minnesota; offenses committed on it may be tried in the courts of either state. And so, also, where it is the boundary between this state and Iowa. This concurrent jurisdiction on lakes Michigan and Superior, and all rivers that bound the state, is given by the acts of congress which admitted this state and the neighboring states into the union. This concurrent jurisdiction does not depend upon this section of the constitution, but would exist whether it was mentioned in the constitution or not.

. The state has given the counties bordering on lakes Michigan and Superior and the Mississippi river, concurrent jurisdiction for offenses committed on these waters; and also to all the counties bordering on lake Winnebago for all offenses committed on that lake.

²The state of Wisconsin guarantees by this clause of the constitution, that all the waters over which it has

control shall be free highways. No tolls or duties are charged for any ship or goods owned by citizens of the United States. In practice it is scarcely worth while for the state of Wisconsin to levy tolls or duties on the few foreign ships that come into our ports; so that really the navigable waters of the state are free for the ships and commerce of all nations, so far as the state is concerned. The United States, however, charge certain tonnage duties on foreign vessels and a tariff on foreign goods brought here, but these duties are the same for all parts of the country, and when foreign vessels or foreign goods have once paid these duties, they are free to go anywhere in the United States. The navigable waters of Wisconsin are thus free highways for the commerce of all the world, subject only to the duties on foreign commerce which congress imposes.

SECTION II.

The title of all lands and other property, which have accrued to the the territory of Wisconsin, by grant, gift, purchase, forfeiture, escheat, or otherwise, shall vest in the state of Wisconsin.

This section belongs logically under article XIV, which regulates the change of Wisconsin from a territory to a state, and substantially the same thing is given over again in one of the clauses of XIV, 4. The state of Wisconsin is the same political body as the territory of Wisconsin, only with a more perfect government, and with larger powers. It, therefore, holds all the property held by the territory.

This title to property may come by a grant from the United States, or some other state, by gift from cities, towns, villages or private persons, as when land is given for public buildings, by purchase, by forfeiture, as when a man buys land of the state and fails to pay for it, in which case it is forfeited to the state, or by escheat, in case any one dies without heirs and his property goes to the state.

SECTION III.

[1] The people of the state, in their right of sovereignty, are declared to possess the ultimate property in and to all lands within the jurisdiction of the state; [2] and all lands, the title to which shall fail from a defect of heirs, shall revert or escheat to the people.

[1] The right of eminent domain is claimed by all civilized governments. The state has the ultimate title to all land within its boundaries, and can take any land from its owner if it is needed for public purposes, only it must pay a fair price for it. (I, 13.) This right belonged to the United States, but when congress admitted this state to the union it gave this right of ultimate sovereignty to the state.

This right of eminent domain is exercised whenever the land needed for any public buildings cannot be purchased, whenever a road or street or a public park is laid out, and whenever a railroad or canal is constructed. In the latter case, the railroad or canal is a public highway; owned and constructed by a private corporation, it is true, but operated for the public benefit, and liable to be controlled by law or to be taken from its owners, should they abuse their trust. Private property can be taken for railroads and canals only because they are *public highways.**

*" In case of a railroad owned by a private corporation in whose favor tne eminent domain may be exercised, the publ'c use consists in the right of the public to the carriage of persons and property upon tender of a proper consideration, and *in the power of the state to control the franchise and limit the tolls.*" (Wis. Reports, vol. xxv, p. 167.)

This right of eminent domain is the right of a sovereign—in this country the sovereign people—and it is meant to be used only for the public good. Highways for commerce are an absolute necessity of any civilized society. But for land transportation artificial highways must be made. These have now come to be railways, wherever railways can be built. These railways could not be built if they had to buy the right of way of each land owner at his own price. The state, therefore, very justly uses the right of eminent domain to take the land needed for railways at a fair price. This is done for the public good. But as the practical monopoly of the carrying trade enjoyed by the railways is very liable to be misused for the injury of the public, the state has rightly reserved the right to control these chartered monopolies (XI, 1), whenever it is necessary to do so for the public good. They are allowed to exercise the sovereign right of eminent domain only for the public good. But they do not have this privilege given to them without any duties in return. They are to use the great powers given to them for the public good. Should they fail to do so, the state can limit their powers or destroy them altogether. They are the servants of the people, the creatures of the state, not its masters and rulers.

[2] In accordance with the same right when any one dies and leaves no heirs his property goes to the state. Land only is spoken of in this section, but the same principle applies to all property.

Any property that thus escheats to the people goes into the school fund. (X, 2.)

ARTICLE X.

EDUCATION.

Sec.

1. OFFICERS, { State Superintendent, - - - -
Such other officers as the legislature directs, - } 1

2. SCHOOL FUND,

Sources,
1. Lands granted by the United States, - - -
2. Property forfeited or escheated, - - -
3. Military exemptions, -
4. Net proceeds of penal fines,
5. All unspecified grants to the state, - - -
6. Five hundred thousand acres of land, - - -
7. Five per cent of the net proceeds of United States land sales, - - } 2

Apportioned,
1. Among the towns and cities of the state, - -
2. In proportion to the school population, - - -
3. Conditions. { That school tax was raised, - That school was maintained three months, } 5

3. SCHOOL TAX, { 1. Annual, - - . - - - - -
2. In each town and city, - - - - - -
3. Not less than half the school fund received, - } 4

4 SCHOOLS
District schools { 1. Uniform, - - -
2. Free to persons of school age, - - - .
3. Unsectarian, - - } 3
Academies and normal schools, - - - - 2

5. UNIVERSITY, { 1. Supported by special grants from the United States, - - - - - - -
2. At or near the capital, - - - - - ·
3. Colleges may be connected with it, - -
4. Unsectarian, } 6

6. SCHOOL LAND COMMISSIONERS,
1. Shall consist of { Secretary of State, -
Treasurer, - - - -
Attorney General,. - - } 7
2. Shall sell, { For cash - -
On time with mortgages. }
3. Shall withhold land from sale in their discretion
4. Shall invest the proceeds as the legislature directs, - - - - - - - -
5. Shall give security, - - - - - - } 8

SECTION I.

[1] The supervision of public instruction shall be vested in a state superintendent, and such other officers as the legislature shall direct. [2] The state superintendent shall be chosen by the qualified electors of the state, in such manner as the legislature shall provide; his powers, duties and compensation shall be prescribed by law. *Provided*, that his compensation shall not exceed the sum of twelve hundred dollars annually.

[1] The state officers who have the supervision of public instruction are an assistant superintendent of public instruction and county and city superintendents. The assistant superintendent is appointed by the state superintendent and performs such duties as he directs. County superintendents are elected for the term of two years, like other county officers. They examine and license teachers, and have the general supervision of the schools and teachers in their respective jurisdictions. Several of the larger counties in the state are divided each into two superintendent districts. The cities have their own systems of school supervision ; generally, under city superintendents, who may or may not be the principals of the high schools. The local supervision of schools is in the hands of the district boards, or where the town system of schools has been adopted, in the hands of the town board of education.

[2] The state superintendent is chosen for a term of two years, at the same time as the other state officers.

SECTION II.

[1] The proceeds of all lands that have been or hereafter may be granted by the United States to this state, for educational purposes, (except the lands heretofore granted for the purposes of a university), and all moneys, and the clear proceeds of all property, that may accrue to the state by forfeiture or escheat, and all moneys which may be paid as an equivalent for exemption

from military duty, and the clear proceeds of all fines collected in the several counties for any breach of the penal laws, and all moneys arising from any grant to the state, where the purposes of such grant are not specified, and the five hundred thousand acres of land to which the state is entitled by the provisions of an act of congress, entitled "an act to appropriate the proceeds of the sale of public lands, and to grant pre-emption rights," approved the fourth day of September, one thousand eight hundred and forty-one, and also the five *per centum* of the net proceeds of the public lands to which the state shall become entitled on her admission into the union, (if congress will consent to such appropriation of the two grants last mentioned,) shall be set apart as a separate fund, to be called the school fund, the interest of which, and all other revenues derived from the school lands, shall be exclusively applied to the following objects, to-wit:

[2] 1. To the support and maintenance of common schools in each school district, and the purchase of suitable libraries and apparatus therefor.

[3] 2. The residue shall be appropriated to the support and maintenance of academies and normal schools, and suitable libraries and apparatus therefor.

[1] A very liberal provision is thus made for a school fund. The following are the sources of that fund:

1. Property which is forfeited or escheated to the state. Property escheats to the state when the owner dies without a will and without heirs.

2. Money paid for exemption from military duty.

3. The net proceeds of all penal fines.

4. All unspecified grants to the state.

5. Section sixteen in each township.

6. The five hundred thousand acres of land first given for the Rock river canal, and afterward by consent of congress given to the school fund.

7. The five per cent. of the net proceeds of the sale of all public lands first given to the state to build roads and canals.

8. One half the proceeds of the swamp lands given to the state by congress in 1850 and 1855   This is now set apart as a normal school fund.

The interest of this fund (except the normal school fund), is apportioned each year among the school districts of the state. This fund now amounts to about two and a half million dollars, and it is constantly increasing, though not so fast as the population of the state increases.

² The interest of the school fund is apportioned to the districts which have maintained school five or more months during the preceding year. This money must be set apart for teachers' wages. The legislature has power under this section of the constitution to furnish libraries and apparatus to the schools out of the school fund; but it has not chosen to do so.

³ Until the year 1859 aid was given by the state to those colleges, academies and high schools which had normal classes of persons intending to teach. Since that time the normal work of the state has been placed in the hands of the Board of Regents of Normal Schools. The income arising from half the proceeds of the swamp lands granted to the state by congress in 1850 and in 1855, is placed at their disposal for the following objects:

1. Building and endowing normal schools. Of these three are now in operation—at Platteville, Whitewater and Oshkosh; and another has been decided upon and will soon be built and in operation at River Falls.

2. Conducting teachers' institutes in the various counties of the state.

3. Conducting normal institutes or movable normal schools in those counties which are too distant from the normal schools to be benefited by them. The money for this last purpose does not come from the school fund, but from the state treasury.

SECTION III.

[1] The legislature shall provide by law for the establishment of district schools, which shall be as nearly uniform as practicable, and such schools shall be [2] free and without charge for tuition to all children between the ages of four and twenty years, and [3] no sectarian instruction shall be allowed therein.

[1] The experience of all modern nations shows that the people must be educated to make the nation strong or fit for freedom. The strength of the German empire is in her schools and universities. The weakness of some other nations of Europe is in the ignorance of the laboring classes. We thus need popular education to make and keep our nation strong, for "knowledge is power."

But we also need popular education to make and keep us fit for freedom. Experience has shown that no nation can long be free unless it is intelligent. It is never the interest of the majority of the people, anywhere, to be oppressed by unjust laws or aristocratic privileges or corrupt governments. Where a whole people is intelligent, even if ruled by no higher motive than self-interest, they will maintain their freedom against military usurpers, corrupt demagogues and wealthy classes and corporations. Those who govern any nation should be intelligent, and in this country where the people are the rulers, the people should be intelligent.*

Another reason for popular education is that the inherent rights of each individual to liberty and the pursuit of happiness, (I, 1) guaranteed by this constitution, may be secured to each one. Every citizen of this state should have a fair chance in life secured to him. And

---

* "The common school, oh, let its light
   Shine through our country's story;
Here lies her health, her wealth, her might;
   Here rests her future glory."

this can only be given by an education which shall fit him to perform intelligently the ordinary duties of life, and that shall give him the clue to all the knowledge possessed by the world. Then if all outside hindrances are removed from his pathway, as they are in this country, each person with this capital of a common school education to start with, can make his own place in life, and be "the architect of his own fortune."

² The common schools in this country are free to all persons of school age, as they are not in any other country in the world. Here the tax payers educate the children of rich and poor alike, believing that " it is cheaper to pay for school houses than to pay for jails and poorhouses."

³ No sectarian instruction is allowed in our schools, for two reasons : first, because we have several different forms of faith in this state, no one of which has a right to have the powerful influence of the schools used in its favor; and second, because the experience of our country has shown that religion thrives best when it is independent of the state, asking no favors from it, and not being controlled by it.*

SECTION IV.

Each town and city shall be required to raise, by tax, annually, for the support of common schools therein, a sum not less than one-half the amount received by such town or city respectively for school purposes, from the income of the school fund.

This tax is assessed by each county on the towns and cities of which it is composed. Towns and cities may

* " Nor heeds the sceptic's puny hands,
　Whilemear her school the church spire stands;
　Nor fears the blinded bigot's rule,
　While near her church spire stands her school."— *Whittier.*

also raise school taxes.* But the greater share of the
school tax is raised by the school districts, each for its
own school.

SECTION V.

Provision shall be made by law for the distribution of the income of the school fund among the several towns and cities of
the state, for the support of common schools therein, in some
just proportion to the number of children and youth resident
therein, between the ages of four and twenty years, and no appropriation shall be made from the school fund to any city or town
for the year in which said city or town shall fail to raise such
tax, nor to any school district for the year in which a school
shall not be maintained at least three months.

The income of the school fund is distributed among
the towns and cities of the state in proportion to the
number of persons between four and twenty years old,
in those districts which have maintained school for *five*
months during the preceding year.

SECTION VI.

[1] Provision shall be made by law for the establishment of a
state university, at or near the seat of state government, and for
connecting with the same from time to time such colleges in
different parts of the state as the interests of education may require. [2] The proceeds of al. lands that have been or may hereafter be granted by the United States to the state for the support
of a universty, shall be and remain a perpetual fund to be called
the "university fund," the interest of which shall be appropriated to the support of the state university, and [3] no sectarian instruction shall be allowed in such university.

[1] The state university has been established at Madison.
No colleges in other parts of the state have yet been
connected with it. The university is governed by a
board of regents, consisting of the state superintendent
and twelve persons appointed by the governor. It is

* "Under the constitution of the state school districts may be organized,
and public moneys raised and apportioned in *villages* as well as in towns and
cities." (Wis. Reports, vol. xxv, p. 465).

open to both sexes, in all its departments. It consists of a "college of letters," a "college of arts," a "female college," an "agricultural college," a "law department," and a "preparatory department."

² In addition to the land grant given by congress for the university, congress in 1862 gave a land grant to each state in the union for agricultural colleges. In this state this grant was given to the state university, for an agricultural college connected with it.

³ No sectarian instruction is allowed in the state university for the same reason that none is allowed in the common schools.

SECTIONS VII AND VIII.

(7). The secretary of state, treasurer, and attorney general shall constitute a board of commissioners for the sale of the school and university lands, and for the investment of the funds arising therefrom. Any two of said commissioners shall be a quorum for the transaction of all business pertaining to the duties of their office.

(8.) Provision shall be made by law for the sale of all school and university lands, after they shall have been appraised, and when any portion of such lands shall be sold, and the purchase money shall not be paid at the time of the sale, the commissioners shall take security by mortgage upon the land sold for the sum remaining unpaid, with seven per cent. interest thereon, payable annually at the office of the treasurer. The commissioners shall be authorized to execute a good and sufficient conveyance to all purchasers of such lands, and to discharge any mortgage taken as security, when the sum due thereon shall have been paid. The commissioners shall have power to withhold from sale any portion of such lands when they shall deem it expedient, and shall invest all moneys arising from the sale of such lands, as well as all other university and school funds, in such manner as the legislature shall provide, and shall give such security for the faithful performance of their duties as may be required by law.

The school fund is thus cared for by a board of three state officers, under the direction of the legislature.

ARTICLE XI.

CORPORATIONS.

This article has been essentially modified by the amendment forbidding special legislation, adopted November
7, 1871. That amendment, which forms section 31 and
32 of article IV, prohibits the legislature from granting
corporate powers or privileges by special laws, except
to cities, and also prohibits the legislature from incorporating any town or village or amending the charter
thereof, by a special law. As it now stands in the constitution the subject of corporations may be analyzed as
follows:

SECTION I.

[1] Corporations without banking powers or privileges may be formed under general laws, but shall not be created by special act, except for municipal purposes, [and in cases where, in the judgment of the legislature, the objects of the corporation cannot be attained under general laws.]* [2] All general laws or special acts enacted under the provisions of this section may be altered or repealed by the legislature at any time after their passage.

[1] By the amendment adopted Nov. 1, 1871, corporate powers cannot now be granted by a special law except to cities. All laws made in regard to corporations, except city charters, must now be general. For instance, all laws chartering insurance companies must apply to all insurance companies. The legislature cannot give one insurance company powers which it refuses to other companies which are doing the same sort of business. So in regard to villages. Every law made about villages must apply to all the villages in the state alike. The legislature cannot give one village powers which it refuses to others. No special charter can now be given to any corporations, either private or municipal, except to cities.

[2] Where the legislature of any state has once given corporate powers without reserve, they cannot be revoked without the consent of the body which receives them.† For instance, if the legislature of this state had

---

* Repealed by the amendment to article IV.

† In the celebrated case of Dartmouth College against Woodward, in which Daniel Webster was attorney for the plaintiff, it was decided by the Supreme Court of the United States that charters are in the nature of a contract, between the government and the corporation, and consequently cannot be altered or repealed by the government without the consent of the corporation, under the U. S. constitution, article I, section 10, which forbids states to pass laws impairing the obligations of contracts. (Wheaton's reports of the U. S. supreme court, vol. vi, p. 518).

But when the constitution of a state reserves the right of repeal, as in this section, all such contracts are made and accepted by the corporations with the right of repeal or amendment by the legislature as one of the im-

given some railroad extraordinary and even dangerous privileges, were it not for this section the legislature could not repeal or alter the charter that gave those extraordinary privileges except with the consent of the railroad. But by this section the legislature can always control all the corporations in the state. And if ,we consider how powerful the great railroad, and telegraph, and express companies and other corporations have grown to be, we shall see how wise is this provision in the constitution. The legislature can now at any time limit the power of these corporations, or even repeal their charters altogether.*

SECTION II.

No municipal corporation shall take private property for public use against the consent of the owner, without the necessity thereof being first established by the verdict of a jury.

If the proper officers of a city, town or village cannot agree with the owner of property which they take for public use, as, for instance, when a street is opened, the owner can call for a jury, who shall decide what the property is worth.

plied conditions of the contract itself, which therefore can be amended or repealed by the legislature at its pleasure. (Wis. Reports, vol. iii, pp. 287 and 611).

"The grant of special franchises made to a corporation by its charter is in the nature of a contract, the obligation of which cannot, under the prohibition of the U. S. constitution, be impaired by subsequent legislation. A state, however, may either by its constitution, as in this state, or by law, reserve the power to repeal or modify any or all such acts of corporation. (Simmons' Digest, p. 120.)

* " In the case of a railroad owned by a private corporation, in whose favor the rights of eminent domain may be exercised, the public use consists in the right of the public to the carriage of persons and property upon tender' of a proper consideration, and *in the power of the state to control the franchise and limit the tolls.*

" Such a qualified and limited public use will not support taxation for the purpose of raising moneys to be *donated* to such a corporation," But counties, cities and villages may become stockholders in a railroad. (Wis. Reports, vol. xxv., p. 16t.)

"The power of the legislature to authorize municipal subscriptions to the stock of railroads is settled by former decisions in this state as well as in other states, though the majority of this court would be disposed to deny the power if it were a new question." (Wis. Reports, vol. xxx., p, 340.)

SECTION III.

It shall be the duty of the legislature, and they are hereby empowered to provide for the organization of cities and incorporated villages, and to restrict their powers of taxation, assessment, borrowing money, contracting debts, and loaning their credit, so as to prevent abuses in assessments and taxation, and in contracting debts by such municipal corporations.

Cities are incorporated by special charters given to each city by the legislature. Villages were, until 1871, incorporated either by special charter or under a general law. But all villages hereafter incorporated must be incorporated under a general law. The financial powers of cities and villages are limited in a great many ways, to prevent abuses in assessments and taxation, too numerous and complicated to be given here. This section of the constitution, however, requires the legislature to limit them in some way.*

SECTIONS IV AND V.

(4.) The legislature shall not have power to create, authorize, or incorporate, by any general or special law, any bank or banking power or privilege, or any institution or corporation, having any banking power or privilege whatever, except as provided in this article.

(5.) The legislature may submit to the voters at any general election, the question of "bank or no bank," and if at any such election a number of votes equal to a majority of all the votes cast at such election on that subject shall be in favor of banks, then the legislature shall have power [to grant bank charters, or] † to pass a general banking law, with such restrictions and under such regulations as they may deem expedient and proper for the security of the bill holders. *Provided*, that no such [grant or] † law shall have any force or effect until the same shall have been submitted to a vote of the electors of the state at some general election, and been approved by a majority of the votes cast on that subject at such election.

* "An act authorizing the city of Kenosha to borrow money and issue bonds or scrip therefor, is void for want of any *limitation* upon the amount of such indebtedness." (Wis. Reports, vol. xxvi., p 23.)

† Repealed by the amendment to article IV.

The amendment which constitutes article IV, sections 31 and 32, of this constitution, annuls so much of these two sections as allow special laws or charters to banks. All banking laws must be general.

Practically, the system of state banks established under this section to issue bank bills, was annulled by the United States when congress established the system of national banks, in 1863.

The United States does not prohibit state banks, and such banks could lawfully be organized in this state now, under the general banking law; but the United States does tax the circulation of all state banks ten per cent., so that they are no longer profitable to carry on; and, therefore, there are no longer any banks in this state or any other state of our union which issue bank bills under state laws.

The office of bank comptroller, which was one of the administrative offices of the state, was abolished in 1869; and the state treasurer attends to what little business still remains to be done in winding up the affairs of the old state banks.

The power to issue bank bills needs to be carefully guarded. Bank bills circulate as money, and are continually passing from hand to hand. Very few people can have the information by which they can tell which are good and which are bad among a great number of banks situated in many states of the union. It was, therefore, right for the state to regulate the whole matter of banking, and throw around it such restrictions as would make bank bills always good, and convertible into gold and silver.

This was a subject on which there were so many opinions, and one of such importance, that the convention which framed the constitution did not attempt to settle it, but left it for the people at the general election in 1851, when it was decided in favor of having banks. A general banking law was passed by the next legislature, and submitted to the people at the general election in 1852, and approved by them. Several amendments have since been made, and each was voted on by the people. Several special charters have also been granted to particular banks, which have been approved of by a vote of the people.

Happily the United States has now taken the whole matter of the currency into its own hands. We now have a national currency, composed of the United States notes, and the notes of the national banks chartered by congress. These are guaranteed by the United States, so that every one who takes one of these bills may be sure that his money is as good as the United States itself. The only banks in this state which now issue bills are national banks. But there are many corporations still in existence with banking powers in every respect, except that of issuing bills.

ARTICLE XII.

AMENDMENTS.

This constitution is subject to the United States constitution, and to the laws, treaties and judicial decisions of the United States, so far as that constitution gives the federal government power over a state ; and, therefore, all amendments made to this constitution must be made subject to the same paramount authority of the United States.

			Sec.
AMENDMENTS MAY BE MADE,	1. *By the legislature,*	By two successive legislatures, - - - - And a vote of the people, -	1
	2. *By convention,*	Proposed by legislature, - Called by vote of the people, - - - - Arranged for by legislature, Elected by vote of the people, - - - -	2

SECTION I.

Any amendment or amendments to this constitution may be proposed in either house of the legislature and if the same shall be agreed to by a majority of the members elected to each ot the two houses, such proposed amendment or amendments shall be entered on their journals with the yeas and nays taken thereon, and referred to the legislature to be chosen at the next general election, and shall be published for three months previous to the time of holding such election. And if in the legislature so next chosen, such proposed amendment or amendments shall be agreed to by a majority of all the members elected to each house, then it shall be the duty of the legislature to submit such proposed amendment or amendments to the people, in such manner and at such time as the legislature shall prescribe, and if the people shall approve and ratify such amendment or amendments by a majority of the electors voting thereon, such amendment or amendments shall become part of the constitution. *Provided,* That if more than one amendment be submitted, they shall be submitted in such manner that the people may vote for or against such amendments separately.

The process of amending the constitution by the leglature is as follows :

1. An amendment may be proposed in either house.

2. The vote must be taken by yeas and nays.

3. The proposed amendment muxt be agreed to by a majority of all the members elected to each house.

4. It must be published for three months before the next general election.

5. It must be agreed to by a majority of all the members of each house in the next legislature.

6. It must be submitted to the people.

7. It must have a majority of all votes cast on that subject.

Ample opportunity is thus given for discussion, and it is not likely that a very unwise measure could run the gauntlet of all the criticism in the legislature and in the newspapers; and certainly no amendment can be passed in this way against the wishes of the people.

It is not necessary that a proposed amendment should have a majority of all the votes cast at that election; but only that it shall have a majority of all cast on that subject.

SECTION II.

If at any time a majority of the senate and assembly shall deem it necessary to call a convention to revise or change this constitution, they shall recommend to the electors to vote for or against a convention at the next election for members of the legislature; and if it shall appear that a majority of the electors voting thereon have voted for a convention, the legislature shall at its next session provide for calling such convention.

It may well happen that the people of the state shall become dissatisfied with the constitution, and wish to have it revised or changed entirely for a new one. In

J

this case it is better to have a constitutional convention called for that special purpose, than to take up the time of the legislature with it. The process of calling a convention to revise or change the constitution is as follows:

1. The legislature may propose a convention, by a joint resolution.

2. The people vote on it at the next general election.

3. If a majority of all the votes cast *on that subject* are for a convention, the next legislature provides for calling it.

4. This convention will be elected by the people at such times and in such a way as the legislature may provide.

5. The convention need not submit its action to the people. A constitution made by such a convention is binding without a vote of the people; for the people have delegated their sovereign power to the members of the convention. But if the legislature in their call of the convention, have prescribed that the constitution shall be submitted to a vote of the people, then the convention was elected, with that limited power of *proposing* a new or revised constitution, but without the power of *making* it. In that case, a vote of the people is necessary, or, if the convention elected with full powers, think best, nevertheless, to submit their work to the people, they have a right so to do; and in that case the new or revised constitution is not binding until ratified by the people's vote.

No constitutional convention has yet been called under this section. The amendments that have been made thus far, have all been made in the way prescribed in the previous section

ARTICLE XIII.

MISCELLANEOUS PROVISIONS.

SECTION I.

[1] The political year for the state of Wisconsin shall commence on the first Monday in January in each year, [2] and the general election shall be holden on the Tuesday succeeding the first Monday in November in each year.

[1] All state officers come into office upon the the first Monday in January, unless they are appointed or elected to fill a vacancy.

[2] At the general election there are chosen, in the even years, representatives in congress, state senators in the odd numbered districts, members of the assembly, and most of the county officers. In the leap years all the above named officers are chosen and in addition to them electors for president and vice president of the United States. In the odd years there are chosen, the governor, lieutenant governor, and all the administra-tive officers of the state, the senators in the even numbered districts, members of the assembly, and a few county officers.

SECTION II.

[1] Any inhabitant of this state who may hereafter be engaged, either directly or indirectly, in a duel, either as principal or accessory, shall forever be disqualified as an elector, [2] and from holding any office under the constitution and laws of this state, [3] and may be punished in such other manner as shall be pro-scribed by law.

[1] A person who has been engaged in a duel is dis-qualified as an elector by that fact. It is not necessary that he should be convicted of the offense in a court of justice. He can be challenged at the polls and put upon

his oath by the inspector of election.   If he swears his vote in falsely, he is liable to be tried for perjury, and sent to the state's prison.   He is also guilty of a misdemeanor for offering to vote, and may be punished for that by fine and a short imprisonment.

[2] Should such a person be elected or appointed to an office, his place could be contested and he be thrown out of office on a writ of *quo warranto* from some court.

[3] Duelling is punished with imprisonment in the state prison, and if any one is killed in a duel it is considered as murder in the second degree and punished accordingly.

SECTION III.

[1] No member of congress, nor any person holding any office of profit or trust under the United States, (postmasters excepted) [2] or under any foreign power; [3] no person convicted of any infamous crime in any court within the United States, and [4] no person being a defaulter to the United States, or to this state, or to any county or town therein, or to any state or territory within the United States, shall be eligible to any office of trust, profit or honor in this state.

This section prohibits different classes of persons from holding office in the state, for very different reasons.

[1] Members of congress and officers of the United States, are prohibited from holding office in this state while they are congressmen or federal office holders, because their duty to the general government would be likely to interfere with their duties to the state.   Members of congress are not United States officers in the strict legal sense of the word, and therefore they are named separately.

Postmasters are excepted; they can hold office under the state, but they cannot be members of the legislature.   (IV, 13.)

[2] Persons holding office under any foreign power are prohibited from holding office here, because they would not be likely to serve two separate governments with loyalty; and cases might easily arise in which the interests of the two governments, and the duties of the two offices would be opposite.

Therefore, officers of foreign powers even when they are our own citizens, as consuls frequently are, are prohibited from holding office in Wisconsin.

[3] No person convicted of an infamous crime anywhere in the United States can hold office in Wisconsin, because he has shown that he is not worthy of trust or honor; and the state would disgrace itself by putting a convicted criminal into a place of honor or trust. The person must have been convicted of the crime in some court; for the law presumes every man innocent till he is proved to be guilty.

[4] No defaulter to any branch of our government anywhere in the United States can hold office, and for the same reasons.

SECTION IV.

It shall be the duty of the legislature to provide a great seal for the state, which shall be kept by the secretary of state; and all official acts of the governor, his approbation of the laws excepted, shall be thereby authenticated.

All appointments to office, all patents for land, all pardons, etc., must have not only the signature of the governor, but the seal of the state, because they are public acts, done by the governor as the executive of the state.

His approbation of the laws is not an executive act, but a legislative one, and, therefore, does not need the seal of the state.

SECTION V.

All persons residing upon Indian lands within any county of the state, and qualified to exercise the right of suffrage under this constitution, shall be entitled to vote at the polls which may be held nearest their residence, for state, United States or county officers. *Provided*, that no person shall vote for county officers out of the county in which he resides.

The Indian lands are not organized into towns, and, therefore, persons living on them are not in any voting precinct. But it would not be fair to deprive them of a vote for other than town officers, as they would be if the rule had no exception, that every elector must vote in the town, village or ward where he resides. Therefore, such qualified electors may vote at the nearest polls for presidential electors, for congressmen and for state officers, and also for county officers, if they live in the county where they vote.

SECTION VI.

The elective officers of the legislature, other than the presiding officers, shall be a chief clerk and a sergeant-at-arms, to be elected by each house.

The lieutenant governor is president of the senate. When he does not preside, for any reason, the senate elects a president from its own members. The assembly elects a speaker from its own members. The chief clerk and the sergeant-at-arms of each house are elected by each house, but are not members and have no vote. The other officers and attendants are appointed. The chief clerk appoints his own assistants and the sergeant-at-arms appoints the postmaster, doorkeepers and firemen. The messengers are appointed by the speaker. The elections are all *vive voce*, and the votes of each member are entered on the journal. (IV, 30)

SECTION VII

No county with an area of nine hundred square miles or less, shall be divided or have any part stricken therefrom, without submitting the question to a vote of the people of the county, nor unless a majority of all the legal voters of the county voting on the question, shall vote for the same.

It is supposed that the area of 900 square miles or 25 congressional townships, is small enough in ordinary cases, for a county. But if the people of the county are willing to divide the county, there is no good reason why they should not.*

SECTION VIII.

No county seat shall be removed until the point to which it is proposed to be removed, shall be fixed by law, and a majority of the voters of the county voting on the question, shall have voted in favor of its removal to such point.

Until the amendment constituting sections 31 and 32 of article IV was adopted the legislature always had to authorize a vote of the people of any county upon the the question of changing the county seat. Hereafter under that amendment that power is taken from the legislature. No special law can be passed, for locat-

---

* In the case of the division of Washington county, the supreme court decided that in computing the area of a county, bodies of water lying within its boundaries are considered parts of the county, and that Washington county could be divided because it then included a part of lake Michigan. (Wis. Reports, vol. iii, p. 200; Simmons' Digest, p. 132).

The supreme court has decided that it is competent for the legislature to enlarge a county which contains less than 900 square miles, by adding to it part of an adjoining county containing a larger area, so that each of them shall be large enough to be divisible without submitting the question to the voters; and by a subsequent act at the same session to form a new county out of territory taken from such adjoining counties, without submitting the question of such division to the voters. (Simmons' Digest, p. 132; Wis. Reports, vol. xvi, p. 343.) This was in the case in the division of Chippewa and Buffalo counties, and the formation of Trempeleau county, in 1864. The legislature has since then several times evaded this section in the same way. The supreme court has also decided that the "voters" meant in this section and the next, are all the legal voters entitled to vote at any election under article iii. The legislature cannot extend or limit the suffrage for the purpose named in these sections. (Simmons' Digest, page 133; Wis. Reports, vol. v, p. 308, and vol. ix, p. 270.)

ing or changing any county seat, but a general law has been passed which covers this whole subject. Before a county seat can be changed, two things must be done The point to which it is to be moved, must be definitely fixed and a majority of all the votes cast on that question must be for changing it to said definite point.*

SECTION IX.

All county officers whose election or appointment is not provided for by this constitution, shall be elected by the electors of the respective counties, or appointed by the boards of supervisors, or other county authorities, as the legislature shall direct. All city, town and village officers, whose election or appointment is not provided for by this constitution, shall be elected by the electors of such cities, towns and villages, or of some division thereof, or appointed by such authorities thereof as the legislature shall designate for that purpose. All other officers whose election or appointment is not provided for by this constitution, and all officers whose offices may hereafter be created by law, shall be elected by the people, or appointed, as the legislature may direct.

Nearly all the officers named above are elected by the people.†

SECTION X.

The legislature may declare the cases in which any office shall be deemed vacant, and also the manner of filling the vacancy where no provision is made for that purpose in this constitution.

Any office is made vacant by the death or resignation of the person holding it, or by his removal from the state,

---

* The legislature may impose conditions precedent to the removal of a county seat, in addition to those imposed by the state constitution.
"A condition that after a majority of votes have been cast (at an election duly held on that question) in favor of the removal of a county seat to a certain city, it shall not be removed until said city shall place at the control of the county supervisors a specified sum of money, is valid." (Wis. Reports, vol. xxiv., p. 49.)

† "An office created by act of legislature may be abolished in like manner, or the term of the officer otherwise shortened by general legislation, after his election, in the absence of any special provision of the constitution forbidding it." (Wis. Reports, vol. xxvi.. p. 428.)

or by his accepting an office from a foreign power, or from the United States. All civil officers can be removed by impeachment, and some officers can be also removed in a shorter way, as judges, by address, and most county officers by the governor. When an officer is so removed his office is vacant. Vacancies are filled in various ways. A vacancy in the office of governor is filled by the lieutenant governor, immediately, and if he also goes out of office, by the secretary of state (V, 7 and 8). Vacancies in the judicial and administrative offices of the state are filled by appointment of the governor till the next election. Vacancies in the legislature are filled by special election, called as soon as possible. Vacancies in the office of superintendent of schools are filled by appointment of the state superintendent. Vacancies in town offices are filled by special election. Vacancies in district boards are filled by appointment by the board or by the town clerk, till the next regular school meeting.

ARTICLE XIV.

SCHEDULE.

SECTION I.

That no inconvenience may arise by reason of a change from a territorial to a permanent state government, it is declared that all rights, actions, prosecutions, judgments, claims and contracts, as well of individuals as of bodies corporate, shall continue as if no such change had taken place, and all process which may be issued under the authority of the territory of Wisconsin, previous to its admission into the union of the United States, shall be as valid as if isssued in the name of the state.

All private rights and claims are thus secured against any question that might be raised upon the technical point that the state of Wisconsin is a different political body from the territory of Wisconsin, and that what had been done in the courts of the territory could not be recognized by the courts of the state. Such a plea would not have been sustained in the higher courts of the state,* but if raised in the lower courts it might have caused some unjust decisions and much inconvenience ; consequently, it is said in plain terms in the constitution itself, so that no one can mistake it.

SECTION II.

All laws now in force in the territory of Wisconsin, which are not repugnant to this constitution, shall remain in force until they expire by their own limitation, or be altered or repealed by the legislature.

It would not do to leave the state without a code of laws until the legislature had adopted one. So the laws of the territory with which the people were already provided, were by this section adopted as the laws of the state, subject to repeal, or amendment, or expiry by their own limitation, like any other laws except that now this constitution became the supreme law of the state and all statutes had to give way to it, whether they were made before or after its adoption.

SECTION III.

All fines, penalties, or forfeitures accruing to the territory of Wisconsin, shall inure to the use of the state.

The state succeeds to the territory as its political heir, and therefore receives all fines and forfeitures that are due the territory. It would not be just that these fines should be remitted to the persons from whom they were due, merely because the government was changed in its form. (See note under section I.)

---

*The supreme court has decided that a change in the form of a government does not extinguish its obligation or destroy private right of property existing at the time of such change. But when a change of government occurs. either in its form or in the person of its ruler, the new government succeeds to the fiscal right and is bound to fulfill the fiscal obligations of the former government. (Simmons' Digest, page 118. See, also, Wis. Reports, vol. ix., p. 41. and Wheaton's Elements of International Law, p. 63.) This is the universal decision of the courts of all civilized countries.

SECTION IV.

[1] All recognizances heretofore taken, or which may be taken before the change from a territorial to a permanent state government, shall remain valid, and shall pass to, and may be prosecuted in the name of the state, and all bonds executed to the governor of the territory, or to any other officer or court in his or their official capacity, shall pass to the governor or state authority, and their successors in office, for the uses therein respectively expressed, and may be sued for and recovered accordingly; [2] and all the estate or property, real, personal or mixed, and all judgments, bonds, specialities, choses in action, and claims or debts of whatsoever description, of the territory of Wisconsin, shall inure to and vest in the state of Wisconsin, and may be sued for and recovered in the same manner and to the same extent, by the state of Wisconsin, as the same could have been by the territory of Wisconsin. [3] All criminal prosecutions and penal actions which may have arisen, or which may arise before the change from a territorial to a state government, and which shall then be pending, shall be prosecuted to judgment and execution in the name of the state. [4] All offenses committed against the laws of the territory of Wisconsin, before the change from a territorial to a state government, and which shall not be prosecuted before such change, may be prosecuted in the name and by the authority of the state of Wisconsin, with like effect as though such change had not taken place; and all penalties incurred shall remain the same as if this constitution had not been adopted. [5] All actions at law, and suits in equity, which may be pending in any of the courts of the territory of Wisconsin, at the time of the change from a territorial to a state government, may be continued and transferred to any court of the state which shall have jurisdiction of the subject matter thereof.

[1] Recognizances and bonds are written pledges given to the state through some officer legally authorized, that some particular thing shall be done or else the person who gives the recognizance or bond will forfeit a certain sum of money named in the bond. A recognizance is given by a person charged with some offense, when he either pledges himself to appear at such a time and stand trial, or pledges himself to keep the peace. Bonds are given by all public officers who handle public money as pledges of their honesty. Bonds are also given by friends of such public officers for their hon-

esty. Bail bonds are given by friends of prisoners pledging themselves that they will appear and stand their trial.

It would not be right that any one should escape the obligation of his bond merely because the form of government was changed. So this section provides that all bonds and recognizances shall remain valid, and if any are forfeited they may be collected just as they would have been before the state government was organized. (See note under section I.)

' The state of Wisconsin is really the same political body, with another name and another form of government, as the territory of Wisconsin. All property that belonged to the territory therefore still continued to belong to the state. The things ennumerated above, are all the different sorts of property which the law recog· nizes. *Real estate* is land with all the buildings and improvements attached to it. *Personal property* is all movable property of any sort. *Mixed property* is that which is partly real and partly personal. *Judgments* are claims against any one, which have been sued out before a court, and which the court has ordered to be collected. *Bonds* are pledges to pay a certain sum of money unless something else is done. *Specialties* are securities for debt, like mortgages. *Choses in action* are rights to something not possessed, but which can be recovered by law. In brief, everything that the territory owned, or claimed, is owned or claimed by the state· (See note under section I.)

' Offenders who were being prosecuted when the changes of government took place, could not plead that the prosecutions begun by the territory could not be carried on by the state, and so go clear of punishment on a technicality. That plea is barred by this section. *Nor could offenders who had not yet been prosecuted escape on a like plea. But *ex post facto* laws are unlawful under the United States' constitution, as well as under this constitution; and therefore the penalties for crimes and misdemeanors committed under the territorial government, were to be such as the territorial law prescribed. although prosecuted by the state.

⁵ Lawyers distinguish between actions at law and suits in equity. The distinction is practically abolished in this state. In common language both are called law suits. To save all trouble the constitution provides that all lawsuits going on at the time of the change in the power of government, shall proceed exactly as if the change had not been made.

SECTION V.

All officers, civil and military, now holding their offices under the authority of the United States, or of the territory of Wisconsin, shall continue to hold and exercise their respective offices until they shall be superseded by the authority of the state.

It is a general principle of law that all officers shall hold office until their successors are elected and qualified. There must be somebody in the offices, or all the machinery of government will be stopped. On the same principle this section provided that all the territorial officers should hold over until their successors were elected and qualified.

SECTION VI.

The first session of the legislature of the state of Wisconsin shall commence on the first Monday in June next, and shall be held at the village of Madison which shall be and remain the seat of government until otherwise provided by law.

At the same time the state officers were inaugurated and the state government was thus organized. The village of Madison, now a city, is still the capital of Wisconsin.

SECTION VII.

All county,precinct and township officers shall continue to hold their respective offices, unless removed by competent authority, until the legislature shall, in conformity with the provisions of this constitution, provide for the holding of elections to fill such offices respectively.

In some of the southern counties of the state the towns were then called precincts. No change was to be made in county or town officers by the transition from territory to state, until the legislature passed laws to carry into effect the provisions of the constitution.

SECTION VIII.

The president of this convention shall, immediately after its adjournment, cause a fair copy of this constitution, together with a copy of the act of the legislature of this territory, entitled "an act in relation to the formation of a state government in Wisconsin, and to change the time of holding the annual session of the legislature," approved October 27th, 1847, providing for the calling of this convention, and also a copy of so much of the last census of this territory as exhibits the number of its inhabitants, to be forwarded to the president of the United States, to be laid before the congress of the United States at its present session.

This was done, and congress approved of this constitution, and admitted the state to the union, May 29, 1848· The members of congress immediately took their seats in the house of representatives, and when the legislature met it elected two senators who took their seats at the next session. The copy of the census was to assure congress that the new state had a large enough population to entitle it to two representatives in congress and four presidential electors that fall.

SECTION IX

[1] This constitution shall be submitted at an election to be held on the second Monday in March next, for ratification or rejection, to all white male persons· of the age of twenty-one years or upwards, who shall then be residents of this territory and citizens of the United States, or shall have declared their intention to become such in conformity with the laws of congress on the subject of naturalization; and all persons having such qualifications shall be entitled to vote for or against the adoption of this constitution, and for all officers first elected under it. And if the constitution be ratified by said electors, it shall become the constitution of the state of Wisconsin. On such of the ballots as are for the constitution, shall be written or printed the word "yes;" and on such as are against the constitution, the word "no." [2] The election shall be conducted in the manner now prescribed by law, and the returns made by the clerks of the boards of supervisors or county commissioners (as the case may be) to the governor of the territory, at any time before the tenth of April next. And in the event of the ratification of this constitution, by a majority of all the votes given, it shall be the duty of the governor of this territory to make proclamation of the same, and to transmit a digest of the returns to the senate and assembly of the state, on the first day of their session. An election shall be held for governor and lieutenant governor, treasurer, attorney general, members of the state legislature, and members of congress, on the second Monday of May next, and no other or further notice of such election shall be required.

[1] A constitution framed by a convention which met the year before, had been rejected by a vote of the people, but this was accepted.

Notice that the qualifications for voters at this election are not the same as those given in article III, of the constitution. Voters were not required to have lived a year in the territory. Only whites were allowed to vote. There was no qualification because of felony or other crimes named in article II, of this constitution. So it came about that some persons were entitled to vote at this election who were not entitled to vote at the next, and some persons were not entitled to vote at this election who were entitled to vote at the next. For instance, civilized Indians could not vote this election but did vote at the next, while white men who had just come to the territory did vote at this election but could not vote at the presidential election held the next fall. But the most of the voters remained the same.

² Provision is thus made for conducting the election, canvassing the elections and making known the result.

SECTION X.

Two members of congress shall also be elected on the second Monday of May next; and [until otherwise provided by law, the counties of Milwaukee, Waukesha, Jefferson, Racine, Walworth, Rock, and Green shall constitute the first congressional district, and elect one member; and the counties of Washington, Sheboygan, Manitowoc, Calumet, Brown, Winnebago, Fond du Lac, Marquette, Sauk, Portage, Columbia, Dodge, Dane, Iowa, La Fayette, Grant, Richland, Crawford, Chippewa, St. Croix, and La Pointe, shall constitute the second congressional district, and shall elect one member.]*

This state has now eight members of congress. The districts have been changed twice since this constitution was adopted, and are now eight in number, to correspond with the number of members.

SECTION XI.

¹ The several elections provided for in this article shall be conducted according to the existing laws of the territory. *Provided*, that no elector shall be entitled to vote, except in the town, ward, or precinct where he resides. The returns of election, for senators and members of assembly, shall be transmitted to the clerk of the board of supervisors, or county commissioners, as the case may be, and the votes shall be canvassed, and certificates of election issued, as now provided by law. [In the first senatorial district, the returns of election for senator shall be made to the proper officer in the county of Brown; in the second senatorial district, to the proper officer in the county of Columbia; in the third senatorial district, to the proper officer in the county of Crawford; in the fourth senatorial district, to the proper officer in the county of Fond du Lac; and in the fifth senatorial district to the proper officer in the county of Iowa.] ² The returns of election for state officers and members of congress, shall be certified and transmitted to the speaker of the assembly at the seat of government, in the same manner as

---

*The words enclosed in brackets are obsolete by their own limitation.

K

the votes for delegates to congress are required to be certified and returned, by the laws of the territory of Wisconsin, to the secretary of said territory, and in such time that they may be received on the first Monday in June next; and as soon as the legislature shall be organized, the speaker of the assembly and the president of the senate shall, in the presence of both houses, examine the returns, and declare who are duly elected to fill the several offices hereinbefore mentioned, and give to each of the persons elected, a certificate of his election.

[1] The manner of election was to be in the usual and familiar way; except that no elector could vote out of the election precinct in which he resided. So that persons living on Indian lands could not vote at this election, although under the constitution (XIII, 5) they are now entitled to vote at the nearest polls.

[2] The returns of the election are specially provided for, as this election is a state election before the state is organized. The returns are not now made and canvassed in that way. (See notes on article V, section 3.)

SECTION XII.

Until there shall be a new apportionment, the senators and members of the assembly shall be apportioned among the several districts, as hereinafter mentioned, and each district shall be entitled to elect one senator or member of the assembly, as the case may be.*

This apportionment has been altered every five years since the constitution was adopted (IV. 3). So that the apportionment given in this section has been long since abolished. Any legislative manual for the current year will give the present senatorial and assembly districts.

This section established nineteen senate districts and sixty-six assembly districts, while the constitution allows as many as thirty-three of the one, and one hundred of the other. The number of senators and assemblymen was increased at each apportionment as the state grew

* As this apportionment is no longer in force, and would take up too much room, it is omitted.

in population, till in 1862 the state legislature had the highest number of members possible, as the constitution now stands. This number is still kept up, and probably will be for many years to come.

SECTION XIII.

Such parts of the common law as are now in force in the territory of Wisconsin, not inconsistent with this constitution, shall be and continue part of the law of this state until altered or suspended by the legislature.

The common law is all that body of customs, precedents and forms which have grown up in England, but which are not expressed in the statutes. It is the unwritten law, as the statutes are the written law. The United States having been colonies of Great Britain adopted, as colonies, and afterwards as states, the common law of England, as the basis of their system of law. Of course, unwritten law can never have the force of written law; and if the two conflict the written law—the constitution and the statutes of the state—will stand, and the unwritten law—the common law—must give way.

Even if this section had not been in the constitution, the courts would undoubtedly have decided that the common law is in force in this state, so far as it is not suspended by the constitution and statutes of the state.*

For the common law has been accepted by the United States courts, and was, therefore, a part of the law governing the territory of Wisconsin, and it would remain a part of the law of the state, except so far as it was ex-

---

* "Both the ordinance of 1787, providing for the government of the northwestern territory, and the constitution of this state, assume and recognize the common law as existing here: and that law, as it existed in England at the time of the American revolution, modified and amended by acts of parliament passed prior thereto, is still in force here, so far as it is applicable to our situation, consistent with our constitution and not repealed by our legislation." (Simmons' Digest, p. 114; Wis. Reports, vol. xviii, p. 147).

pressly abrogated. But, to avoid all controversy this is
stated in the constitution, so that no one can mistake it.

SECTION XIV.

The senators first elected in the even numbered senate districts,
the governor, lieutenant governor, and other state officers first
elected under this constitution, shall enter upon the duties of
their respective offices on the first Monday of June next, and
shall continue in office for one year from the first Monday of January next. The senators first elected in the odd numbered senate
districts, and the members of the assembly first elected, shall
enter upon their duties respectively on the first Monday of June
next, and shall continue in office until the first Monday in January next.

The members of assembly and the senators in the odd
districts were to hold office for seven months, the rest of
the year. The senators in the even districts and the
state officers were to hold office for the rest of the year
and one year more. After the first election, assemblymen were to be chosen every year; the state officers,
and the senators in the even districts in the odd years;
and the senators in the odd districts in the even years.

SECTION XV.

The oath of office may be administered by any judge or justice
of the peace, until the legislature shall otherwise direct.

The constitution directs that members of the legislature and most officers, shall take an oath of office,
swearing that they will support the constitution of the
United States and of the state of Wisconsin, and faithfully discharge the duties of the offices to the best of their
ability. (IV, 28.) This section provides that the oath
may be administered by any judge or justice of the
peace until the legislature otherwise directs. Various
other officers are now allowed to administer the oath of
office.

APPENDIX.

SUGGESTIONS TO TEACHERS.

This text book is designed to *aid* in teaching the constitution of our state, but not to *take the teacher's place.* Merely hearing recitations committed to memory from the pages of this book or reading it over with the pupils, will not amount to much. Only thorough teaching, by a teacher who is full of the subject to be taught and who understands the right methods of instruction, will ever accomplish much with any branch of learning, and especially with a study so abstract and technical as the consti. tution.

I. ORAL TEACHING.

This method can be followed in every school in which there are pupils above the primary grade. A few minutes each day can easily be devoted to a general exercise upon the constitution of the United States or the constitution of the state of Wisconsin. This is the only method by which these subjects can be success-fully taught, except with advanced scholars.

1. MATTER.— What shall be taught in these general exercises? The object of the law requiring these constitutions to be taught is not to make lawyers or politicians, but *intelligent citizens.* Therefore, only such parts of the constitution should be taught in these general exercises as will teach the children the spirit and objects of our government and its general frame work. Bearing this in mind, any teacher can go through the constitu. tion and select the knowledge which is of value to voters and citizens, and arrange it to suit himself. For the benefit of those

teachers who do not care to do this, a series of questions for oral exercises is placed at the close of these " Suggestions to Teachers." These questions should not be followed blindly, but should be changed in their form and in their order to suit the needs of each school;. some questions may be omitted and others inserted at the discretion of the teacher. In short, these questions should be used as a *staff*, not as a *crutch*.

2. MANNER.— How shall the teaching be conducted in these general exercises? In accordance with the nature of children.

Each lesson should be *short*, because children like variety, and dislike long and tedious exercises.

The teaching should be done in a *lively* and *interesting* manner, because children like vivacity and dislike dullness.

What has already been taught should be *constantly reviewed*, because children learn only by constant repetition.

Whenever there is a question, the answer to which the children can reasonably be expected to know, ask it of them. Tell them nothing except what they cannot answer themselves. Frequently, a series of shrewd questions will lead children on from something they already know to something they do not know, but which the questions asked them lead up to.

Much interest can sometimes be aroused among the parents as well as among the children by giving out questions for which the children are to find the answers at home from father and brothers.

Some answers should be given in concert and some by individuals, varying the method so as to secure attention, and so as to be certain that *each pupil* knows what has been taught.

Use *simple language* and as many *illustrations* as possible. Children can grasp large ideas, if these are expressed in simple language, and are freely illustrated with examples.

Guard against the common fault of letting pupils learn *words* instead of *ideas*. Vary the form of the questions so as to test whether the pupils have learned the meaning of the answer, or only a form of words for it.

II. TEXT BOOK TEACHING.

This is the proper method for advanced classes, and should be followed wherever a class of advanced pupils can be organized, but not to the neglect of the oral teaching of the constitution to the whole school.

1. MATTER.— The matter to be taught is the whole constitution with as much collateral information relating to the government of Wisconsin as teacher and class can collect. For this consult the Legislative Manual and Taylor's Revised Statutes, and question any good lawyer, well-informed editor, or leading politician. This study of collateral matters will have for the class all the value of original investigation in the stimulus of mental activity. To aid in this a list of topics for collateral study is given on page .74.

2. MANNER.— No questions are given in this work at the foot of the page or at the close of each section; because such ques tions are so likely to be depended on by teacher and pupils. The best method of recitation is not by specific questions and answers upon each point in the lesson, but by a topical recitation corrected by careful cross-examinations.

Topical recitations are the best because they train the pupil into the habit of telling what he knows of any subject without hesitation or embarrassment, and because a much fuller and clearer knowledge of the subject can be shown in this way. A topical recitation is not a repetition of the words of the lesson committed to memory, but it is a clear and connected statement of the facts and ideas of the lesson. With pupils who have not been accustomed to topical recitations, a ready and complete recitation cannot be secured at once, and aid must be given occasionally by specific questions. But such pupils should be aided as little as possible, and should be led along to the right manner of reciting as soon as possible. Every recitation, to be of the greatest benefit to the class, should contain these three parts:

First. A topical recitation by members of the class. If the lessons are short and the class small, it would be advisable to have each member of the class recite the whole lesson. When this is not the case, it would be well to secure the attention of the class by requiring each pupil to be ready to take up the recitation wherever it may be left, and to go on with it. As little help as possible should be given to the pupil reciting, and he should not be interrupted · by needless questions before he is through. A written analysis of the lesson is a good form of a topical recitation. With a large class it would be well to send a part to the blackboard to make an analysis of the lesson, while the rest are reciting. Or, an analysis on slates or on paper may be brought to the class. The analysis given in this work at the head of each article should not be strictly adhered to, or else the danger of all memorizing will beset the class, that they will fail to think for themselves, and will learn words and forms instead of ideas. It would be well to require of the class an original analysis of each important section. A specimen of such an analysis is given on page 23.

Second. The knowledge of the subject thus shown by a topical recitation should be still further tested by a series of shrewd cross-questions. These questions should be adapted to test how far the pupil has learned ideas, and how far he has only learned words. This can be tested by putting a question in a different form of words from those in which the statement is made in the book; but words which mean the same thing. These questions should also be adapted to stimulate thought, and to test the pupil's power of thought. This can be done by questions, the answers to which are not directly given in the book, but which can be fairly deduced from statements made there. It is well to leave some questions open occasionally from one recitation to the next for the class to investigate in the meantime.

Third. Oral instruction should be given by the teacher on all subjects which the class should know, but which they cannot learn for themselves. If the teacher has seen the legislature in session, or has been present at a term of a circuit court, or has watched closely all the proceedings at an election, or has visited the capitol or any of the state institutions, he can give the class a word picture of what he has seen, which will interest and in-

struct them. Some of the collateral information called for by
the topics given on page 174, can be told by the teacher to the
class, and some of it can be found by them under the teacher's
guidance.

But it should be borne in mind that it is a fact of human nature, true of both children and adults, that we remember what
we have found out for ourselves much better than what some one
else has found out for us, and that we are more deeply im-
pressed with what we ourselves have said than with what some
one else has told us. The teacher should not be satisfied, therefore, with talking to his class. He should fix in their minds his
oral instruction by questioning them upon it until they can tell
it to him understandingly; and he should not suffer two or three
bright scholars to do all the reciting, while the rest only listen.

In places where a debating society can be sustained by advanced pupils and citizens, it will often be found interesting
and profitable to organize such a society as a legislative assembly, or a "mock legislature." To carry on such a mock legislature with profit and interest, the forms of a real legislature should
be somewhat simplified in details. Only one house should be
organized. The rules of the assembly should be adopted and
followed so far as the limitations of time and numbers will allow.
Care should be taken not to spend too much time wrangling over
points of order. The legislative manual will furnish all the information needed to begin and carry on such a mock legislature.
If carried on as it should be this plan will not only furnish a
varied field for debaters, young and old, but it will help to create
an intelligent interest in the workings of our representative government.

QUESTIONS FOR ORAL TEACHING.

These questions should be regarded as suggestive only, and should be varied to suit the needs of the school. Only a few should be taken for a lesson, and these should be made the basis of a great variety of collateral questions which can easily be invented by an ingenious teacher. Constant reviews are necessary. The teacher should on no account use a book in conducting these oral exercises.

1. In what town do you live (or village or city, as the case may be)?
2. In what county do you live?
3. Bound the county. Point it out on the map
4. In what state do you live?
5. Bound Wisconsin. (See page 41.)
6. Point it out on the map.
7. What is Wisconsin? (A state.)
8. Of what country is it a part?
9. What composes the state of Wisconsin? (The land and the people who live on it.)
10. Are you a part of the state of Wisconsin then?
11. Why? (Because we are people and we live in the state.)
12. Who governs the state of Wisconsin? (The people.)
13. What do you call the sort of government in which the people govern? (A democracy.)
14. What three kinds of government are there?
15. What is a monarchy? (A country where one man governs.)
16. What is an aristocracy? (A country where a few men rule all the rest.)
17. What is a democracy? (A country where the people govern themselves.)

18. Which is the best government to have?*

19. You say the people of Wisconsin govern themselves. Do they get together in one place and make the laws? (No; they choose men to make the laws for them.)

20. And when the laws are made how are they carried out? (The people choose officers to carry out the laws.)

21. You say the people choose their law-makers and officers. Who are the people of Wisconsin? (Every man, woman and child in the state.)

22. Then are you a part of the people of Wisconsin?

23. Do you help to choose these law-makers and officers?

24. Why not? (Because we are not voters.)

25. Who are the voters? (The men over 21 years old, who have lived in the state a year.)†

26. What do the voters do? (They choose men to make the laws, and others to carry them out.)

27. What body of men is it that makes the laws?

28. Of what two houses does the legislature consist?

29. How are assemblymen elected?

30. For how long?

31. What qualifications must they have?

32. How are senators elected?

33. For how long?

34. What qualifications must they have?

35. How many assemblymen are there?

36. How many senators are there?

37. How often does the legislature meet?

---

*Here the teacher should enlarge upon the blessings of liberty, and should tell the children what we owe to our free institutions. Because we live in a free country we are safe in life and limb. No one dares kill or hurt us; or if he does, he is punished for it. We can travel where we please. We can engage in any business we are fit for. and be respected for what we really are and do. Our children can go to school and have a chance to be somebody. If we have bad laws we have only ourselves and the rest of the people of the state to blame for it. If we want the laws changed we must persuade the rest of the people of the state to help us change them.

This should be told little by little. and not merely *told* but *taught*, by constant questions and answers, and by frequent illustrations, till the children really understand the blessings of freedom which we enjoy.

The children should be taught to sing patriotic songs in connection with the oral exercises and to understand their meaning.

†Minor distinctions should be omitted. The teacher should warn the scholars that the answer given above is not quite right, but that it is near enough right for all practical purposes.

38. Where does it meet?
39. Suppose you want to have a certain law passed, what must you do? (We must get some senator to introduce it into the senate, or some assemblyman to introduce it into the assembly.)
40. What must be done with it next? (It must be agreed to by the senate or the assembly, whichever it was in which the bill was introduced.)
41. What next? (It must be sent to the other house and agreed to by that house.)
42. Suppose either the senate or the assembly refuses to agree to it, what then?
43. If it passes both houses, what next? (It goes to the governor for his signature.)
44. If he signs it, what then? (It becomes a law.)
45. If he does not sign it, what then? (It goes back to the legislature. If two-thirds of each house vote for it, it becomes a law in spite of the governor.)
46. In whom is the executive power vested?
47. How is the governor elected?
48. For how long?
49. What qualifications must the governor have?
50. If the governor dies, or resigns, or is removed from office by impeachment, who takes his place?
51. If the governor is sick or goes out of the state, what then?
52. How is the lieutenant governor elected?
53. For how long?
54. What qualifications must he possess?
55. What are the administrative officers of the state?
56. How are they all elected?
57. For how long?
58. What qualifications must they have?
59. What does the secretary of state do? (He keeps the records of the state.)
60. What does the state treasurer do? (He keeps the money and accounts of the state.)
61. What does the attorney general do? (He is the lawyer for the state.)

61. What does the superintendent of public instruction do? (He has charge of all the schools in the state.)
62. What does the commissioner of immigration do? (He invites foreigners to come here, and finds places for them when they come.)
63. In whom is the judicial power vested? (In the courts.)
64. What are the principal courts in the state? (The supreme court and the circuit courts.)
65. What is the supreme court composed of?
66. What are the circuit courts composed of? (One judge in each circuit.)
67. How are all these judges elected?
68. For how long?
69. What qualifications must they have?

TOPICS FOR COLLATERAL STUDY.

1. The history of Wisconsin.
2. The first constitution of the Northwest territory (given in the ordinance of 1787, for which see Taylor's Revised Statutes).
3. The history of the present constitution.
4. The origin of trial by jury and *habeas corpus.*
5. The origin of the individual rights guaranteed in article I. (See any good history of England, especially Hallam's Constitutional History of England. See also, Blackstone's and Kent's commentaries.)
6. What feudal tenures were, and the oppressions of the feudal lords. (See Hallam's Middle Ages and Guizot's History of Civilization.)
7. The history of religious freedom in the United States.
8. The United States survey of land in Wisconsin, describing the principal meridian, townships, ranges, sections, quarter sections, etc., with the errors in the surveys and their causes.
9. The manner of conducting an election, and of counting the votes and canvassing the returns.
10. In what senate district are you? In what assembly district? In what congressional district? In what judicial circuit?
11. The rules of parliamentary practice. (See Jefferson's Manual or Cushing's Manual.)
12. The manner of conducting business in the legislature, especially the meaning of the following terms, frequently used in the newspapers: standing committee; special committee; reference to a committee: first, second and third readings; suspension of the rules; call of the house; general file; committee of the whole; previous question; minority report; adjourn; lay on the table; motion to reconsider; amendment.

13. Powers and duties of the state officers.

14. Manner of applying to the governor for a pardon.

15. Powers and duties of the various county officers.

16. Manner of conducting an impeachment trial.

17. Manner of conducting civil suits in the various courts.

18. Manner of conducting criminal cases.

19. The present financial condition of the state. (See the secretary of state's report, or the legislative manual.)

20. The school system of the state. (See school code.)

21. The present condition of the school fund. Of the university fund. Of the Normal school fund.

22. The condition of your own school district the past year, in regard to the number of children of school age; the number who have attended school; the length of school; the finances, etc. (See the district clerk's report to the town clerk.)

23. The condition of the schools in your town or city, in the same respects. Compare them with other localities. (See state superintendent's report.)

24. The various sorts of corporations organized under general laws; and how organized.

25. The Indian reservations in the state.

26. A list of the counties in the state; the date of their organization, and any changes made in their boundaries since. (See Taylor's Revised Statutes.)

27. The names and locations of the various county seats.

28. The present apportionment of the state into congressional districts.

29. The apportionment into senate and assembly districts. (Take a twenty-five cent map of the state and mark the boundaries of the districts by colored lines, a different color for each of the three apportionments; or if the school has a map of the state, it might be well to mark the apportionments upon it.)

30. The various classes of crimes and misdemeanors, and their punishments.

www.ingramcontent.com/pod-product-compliance
Lightning Source LLC
Chambersburg PA
CBHW030847270326
41928CB00007B/1263